BIPOLAR DISORDER AS A TEEN

DISCOVER 5 PRACTICAL WAYS TO OVERCOME THIS
DISORDER BY CHALLENGING YOUR PERSONAL BEHAVIORS,
REFRAMING NEGATIVE THOUGHTS, AND FINDING RELIEF IN
LIVING LIFE TO THE FULLEST.

NATASHA RAE SIMMONS

STORK
PUBLISHING
HOUSE

TABLE OF CONTENTS

INTRODUCTION

Your teenage years are an extraordinary time, marked by profound growth, moments of wonder, challenges, and great learning. However, when this journey includes dealing with bipolar disorder, the path may take on unique challenges not only for yourself but for your family as a whole. You may find yourself dealing with large mood swings, ranging from mania and depression. Common symptoms of mania include irritability, dangerous choices, risky behavior, elation, euphoria, intensity, and racing thoughts. In moments of depression, you may find yourself dealing with fatigue, decreased energy, and insomnia. Sometimes, the manic episodes may lead to brilliant ideas, wonderful insights, great creativity, and feelings of invincibility. Meanwhile, during a depressive episode, you may find yourself feeling extremely low, anxious, irritable, lacking motivation, and having endless thoughts of worthlessness, hopelessness, and despair.

These drastic shifts in energy and moods can be confusing, overwhelming, and frustrating for you as the person experiencing them, and for the family supporting you. This is why you may have many questions, concerns, and worries about how to live your best, healthiest life. *Bipolar Disorder As A Teen* contains many, if not all, of those commonly asked bipolar-related questions with up-to-date, exhaustively researched, and fact-checked answers. I have no doubt you will find many answers to your questions inside this book.

This book explains, in great detail, the illness known as bipolar disorder, its symptoms, early warning signs, and potential root causes. It talks about the possible effects of bipolar disorder on your life and relationships. It also discusses how you can successfully overcome this disorder by challenging your personal behaviors, reframe negative thoughts, and find relief in living life to the fullest.

This book is designed to be thorough, enlightening, and accurate, while being simple, friendly, and easily digestible. *Bipolar Disorder As A Teen* brings to it a combination of all my years studying mental health in teens and young adults as well as my love for mental health development study as it relates to the applications that suit teens. The subject matter of this book is quite complex and not easy to summarize, so the discussion may come across as lengthy. That is because a bipolar diagnosis is not always light–it's not just a simple list to check off. Its treatment isn't just about the administration of a drug. It goes beyond that.

Research indicates that bipolar disorder is widely genetic and frequently inherited—approximately 80% of the time.[1] However, collectively as a whole, you, me, family, friends, and the community, have a responsibility to participate in its treatment. On the flip side of an inherited disorder is the reality of a family member, such as a parent or a sibling, having it as well, which can complicate treatment. Families play a critical role in bipolar treatment because they have a huge and deep impact on recovery. Family is the cornerstone of emotional development right from the beginning. Family nurtures emotional bonds, promotes positive connections, and enhances positive communication.

It's also true and important to recognize that not everyone's family dynamic is healthy. Not everyone has a supportive family environment or a reliable family setup they can lean on, call on, or count on.

Not all families are built on the premise of unconditional love, mutual respect, and constant support. But
families come in different shapes and forms. A family
can be identified as someone who is there for you,
loves you unconditionally, and supports you no matter
what, but it may not always be biological family
members. For this reason, the terms "loved ones" and
"family" used throughout this text mean your support
system. They may be your parents, siblings, friends,
and guardians, either related or not, through blood or
other bonds, and healthcare providers such as doctors
and therapists.

Research has shown that when a teenager struggling with bipolar disorder is greatly loved and
supported by their family members, they are more
likely to be emotionally stable, keep up with their
medications and appointments, and identify episodes
before they get out of hand. Conversely, an unsup-
portive household and an emotionally charged environment can be as dangerous to recovery as skipping
medication regularly.[2] Yes, the family also plays a
huge part in your journey toward recovery. Later on,
we will touch on the role of family in diagnosis and
treatment.

One of the most important messages of this book
is a truth that often accompanies almost all medical

conditions of this century. You must be informed enough to understand where the issues lie, what questions you must ask, and the limitations of your knowledge base. And because it is always best to be one step ahead of others as it relates to your condition, *Bipolar Disorder As A Teen* is a must-read for a teen living with this disorder. It is also a must-read for parents and siblings of teens and young adults living with this disorder.

This introduction sets the wheel in motion for the transformative and insightful tips you'll read in the next chapters of this book, guiding you as you go through life, while also dealing with the complexities of bipolar disorder. This book is about empowerment–empowering you to recognize the realities of bipolar disorder and its impact on your life and family and taking the right steps toward treatment and recovery. From my experience of working with those individuals struggling with bipolar disorder and other mood disorders, I have learned that teenagers and young adults who find improvement with this disorder are those who have learned to recognize their triggers and find ways to minimize the impact of those triggers on their lives and the loved ones supporting them.

I know of teenagers who keep their prescribed

medication close and have dependable relationships with their healthcare providers. They work with therapists and have strong relationships with their support groups. They love and appreciate their family members who have been the ones standing beside them during *AND* after tough episodes. They are well informed about their condition through reading books, blogs, and articles, listening to podcasts, talking to other people who struggle with the same issues, and attending webinars and conferences. They are always ready to help people who struggle with the same disorder as them. They have learned to accept their condition and even understand that this condition doesn't have to limit them. They have dreams and goals, and they pursue them relentlessly. They are living their lives to the fullest. This is what I want for you.

I'd like you to think of this book as your companion—a loving guide offering assurance and reassurance every step of the way. Think of it as that friendly chat you'd have with a trusted caregiver who understands your worries and knows how to address and solve them regularly. Think of this book as performing the same function as a supportive family who loves and cares for you.

I genuinely hope that after reading this book,

you'll feel less alone in your daily struggles, and understand that there are reliable and effective treatment options out there. Know that you can always turn to the strategies discussed here to help you cope with your condition and prevent the disorder from ruling your life.

I hope this book answers your questions and tells you what needs to be said. I also hope you'll be open and willing to listen, even if you'd rather not hear them. Most importantly, I want to hope that by writing this book and you reading it, a fire will awaken within you: a desire to understand and find out everything there is to know about bipolar disorder, and in doing so, find ways to live a happy, healthy life despite your diagnosis.

Please understand that this book is in no way meant to replace professional help and advice. If you have intense and troublesome mood swings that often impair your ability to function normally—maybe you've been skipping school, have troubled relationships, or have turned to unhealthy coping mechanisms —you need to talk to your doctor or therapist. If you've been diagnosed already, you probably have medication—well, you must stick to it and follow your doctor's advice strictly. If you struggle with thoughts of self-harm, please talk to a trusted adult immediately so you can find appropriate help as soon as possible.

Dealing with a complex condition such as bipolar disorder and learning to navigate life while dealing with its symptoms, can be challenging. It means learning *and* relearning to accept that there may be things you are currently doing that aren't working in your favor and finding ways to change them. In doing that, some people tend to be hard on themselves. They may beat themselves up when they have trouble making changes or relapse into old and destructive patterns. Don't do this to yourself. Give yourself the compassion and empathy you so freely give to others.

Remember that change is hard. So, as you continue working on yourself, don't forget to celebrate yourself, give yourself a pat on the back every time you get something right—no matter how small, and be happy that you are taking the initiative and making an effort toward living a happier, healthier life.

I wish you all the best as you embark on this journey. I hope this book will help you find ways to thrive through the ups and downs of bipolar disorder and all it entails.

CHAPTER 1

WHAT IS BIPOLAR DISORDER?

W e all deal with mood swings from time to time. It's part of being human. But the mood swings related to bipolar disorder are different —they are intense, usually alternating between moments of extreme highs and lows. For this reason, bipolar disorder is often referred to as a mood disorder characterized by four different types of moods—**manic/mania, hypomanic/hypomania, depressed**, and **mixed states**.

The National Alliance on Mental Illness, has documented bipolar disorder as a psychiatric disorder, a mental health condition, or a brain disorder that impacts a person's *"mood, concentration, activity level, sleep patterns, and energy."*[1]

When we look at the details, the term bipolar can be split into two parts:

- Bi—translates to *"two."*
- Polar—means *"complete opposites."*

When loosely translated from these two phrases, bipolar could be taken to mean *"between two extreme states,"* as in two extreme moods—mania and depression. Bipolar disorder was previously called manic depression.[2] This older term is still in use, but to a limited degree. But both phrases—bipolar and manic depression, can be a little misleading. This may have also contributed to the many myths and misconceptions surrounding bipolar disorder.[3]

People may take it that bipolar disorder is all about mood swings that spiral from depression to mania or from mania to depression. I would say bipolar is more complex than this. Bipolar disorder is characterized by extreme moods, but those can vary between mania, depression, and everything in between. Sometimes, you are okay; sometimes, you deal with intense feelings. What's more, you may never experience certain moods. For example, not everyone with bipolar disorder experiences mania. So, one of the best ways to describe bipolar disorder is *"a mood disorder."*[2]

But to fully understand the term "mood disorder," we must first break down what "mood " means here.

This is the first step in truly understanding bipolar disorder. The Cambridge Dictionary describes "mood" as *"how you feel at a particular time."*[4] Not quite helpful, if you ask me. The words "feel" and "at a particular time" may start to capture the idea, but the moods in bipolar disorder are more than just feelings.

Moods include many things—happiness, sorrow, or grief; feelings of contentment or dissatisfaction with life; and even physical feelings such as exhaustion and vigor. Considering these factors, moods become more complex and can be influenced by simple things such as emotional and physical comfort or discomfort.

When you are in a good mood, you feel happy and optimistic about life and the possibilities and are excited about the future. You feel content, relaxed, and friendly. Happy would be the right word to describe how you feel when you are in a good mood. You sleep soundly, eat heartily, are full of energy, and have a positive sense of well-being. When you are in a good mood, the world is wonderful; your friends and family are great people, and you enjoy every minute spent with them. It feels great to be alive and to have this life. When people are in a good mood, they can be friendly and are easily sociable. They are ready to pursue their dreams, chase their goals, and start new projects.

When you are in a bad mood, you experience the opposite of what's described above. When you are unhappy, you may turn inward. You may become preoccupied with your thoughts and may be easily distracted. The phrase "sad" would capture some of it, but it's still insufficient. It's more complicated. You may feel a lot of emptiness when you are in a bad mood. There could be a profound sense of loss. It's hard to think about the future, at least not in a positive way. When you think about the future, you may look at it in a pessimistic way. You may even feel intimidated. You may lose your temper easily and then spend the next few hours feeling guilty for doing so. Being affectionate and sociable becomes hard.

For this reason, others prefer to isolate themselves and sit alone for many hours. As self-doubt takes over, your energy levels may become extremely low. You may become preoccupied with negative thoughts. What's more, you worry about how others perceive you.

The mood swings and changes associated with bipolar disorder are not just simple highs and lows. You see, people who don't have bipolar disorder deal with mood fluctuation, too. However, their mood changes normally last a few hours and not days. The mood changes experienced aren't associated with extreme behavioral changes either. The mood changes in people who don't have bipolar disorder aren't associated with difficulties in daily routines or social interactions. But a bipolar disorder patient's mood swings are so intense they usually disrupt their daily life, relationships, and life in general. The mood changes are so far removed from the normal range that it doesn't take an expert to know something is wrong.

Moreover, the mood changes associated with bipolar disorder are often accompanied by changes in thought patterns and bodily functions. These changes are enough proof that the mood fluctuations related to bipolar disorder are far from normal. These changes include fluctuations in concentration and motivation levels, impaired concentration and memory, extreme insomnia, and low energy levels. It's simply not right to say that a person with bipolar disorder is just dealing with "*extreme mood changes.*" Think of it this way—it's a complex system that doesn't work or at least doesn't work as it should.

Imagine a person whose temperature regulation system is faulty. It's a warm, sunny day, and they start shivering. It's a cold winter day, and they suddenly break out into a sweat. Their reaction to cold and warm weather is completely abnormal. Their body thinks it's cold when it's not or hot when it's not. Now, translate that into a mood regulation problem— bipolar disorder. The body is a little disconnected from the individual's environment. The phrases "happy" or "unhappy" take on completely different forms from what we are used to. Sometimes, the mood fluctuations are so mild they could be dismissed; sometimes, they are so extreme they could be misdiagnosed.

Speaking of misdiagnosis, it's worth noting that bipolar disorder is an umbrella term that covers multiple diagnoses. Let's talk about that.

BIPOLAR AND ITS SUBTYPES

Bipolar disorder is a general term describing a group of mental health issues, including:

- Bipolar I disorder.
- Bipolar II disorder.
- Cyclothymic disorder or cyclothymia.
- Mixed bipolar state.
- Rapid cycling bipolar.
- Other specified bipolar-related disorders.

- Other unspecified bipolar and related disorders.
- Drug and substance-induced bipolar and related disorders.
- Bipolar and related disorders resulting from other medical conditions.
- Co-morbidities—other medical conditions occurring with bipolar.

Mood episodes are the hallmarks of bipolar disorder. The highs are called manic episodes; the lows are called depressive episodes. Please understand that not all forms of bipolar disorders come with depressive episodes. First, let's discuss the episodes in detail.

WHAT IS MANIA?

Manic episode

A manic episode describes a state of mind characterized by euphoria, excitement, high energy, and abnormally elevated moods.[5] A bipolar diagnosis often involves mania. But a manic episode isn't just about feelings of joy and euphoria; you may also find yourself engaging in impulsive behavior, irrational decision-making, grandiosity, and concentration issues. Impulsive behavior may include things like spending huge amounts of money and engaging in high-risk behavior with potentially harmful outcomes.

Euphoria, elevated mood, and high levels of excitement mean you may feel extremely happy about very small things. It's even possible to feel a happy kind of "high" without using any type of drug. Still, it's not always that when you are in a manic episode, you will feel happy and excited. You may be irritable and show extreme agitation, especially if others try to warn you, stop, or stand in your way of doing something extreme.

Impulsive behavior

This type of behavior may manifest in the form of drug and alcohol abuse, unsafe and risky sexual behavior, driving recklessly, driving at dangerously high speeds, exercising to the point of injury, and sometimes, even having artistic and creative binges.

Grandiosity

While in a manic episode, you may entertain thoughts of being "superhuman." You may feel like you have supernatural powers or privileges you don't actually have. While in the midst of a manic episode, you may demand instant gratification for your needs. In the case where you want something, you may demand it now, not later.

You may talk endlessly about new creative projects you've never thought of before and expect them to be fulfilled immediately. You may speak highly of yourself, believing you are some untouchable CEO, a powerful politician, or a spiritual leader, when in reality, you may not be. You may think about starting a business suddenly and randomly, and then try to use all your family's savings to do so, if you can access it.

Fast-talking

When you are in a manic episode, you may talk too fast, be extremely talkative, or both. No, it's not that you are simply speaking quickly; it will seem like you can't get your words out fast enough. This is sometimes called pressure of speech. If you are talking to a person in a manic episode, you may feel like you are almost being pushed and pressed against a wall.

Lack of sleep

Indeed, manic episodes are characterized by high energy levels, but you may be able to operate on very little or no sleep at all.

Distraction

Manic episodes may be characterized by extreme distractions. Your thoughts may start to race, pushing you to multitask. This may manifest as taking on or starting multiple complex projects but not making the effort to complete them.

Psychosis

Sometimes, manic episodes may be characterized by psychosis, which could manifest as hallucinations and delusions. For example, a psychotic episode may lead you to believe that you are a powerful government official, spy, or secret agent well-trained in the craft. You may not be trained, but the psychosis makes you believe you are. You may experience paranoia, too, believing that you are a victim of stalking or targets.

WHAT IS HYPOMANIA?

Hypomania

Hypomania is a less intense or less severe form of mania.[6] Still, the behaviors of a person in a hypomanic episode differ from the normal behaviors of someone who isn't hypomanic. The moods are different from the person's normal moods. These differences will be so extreme that the people around you may notice.

When you are in a hypomanic episode, you may have high levels of energy and operate with little to no sleep as well. You may feel confident but not grandiose, as with mania. You may suddenly take on many new and complex projects and become angry and irritable when someone tries to stop you. You may have difficulty concentrating, but you will still be relentless. This is to say that while a hypomanic episode may be distinct, the symptoms aren't so intense that they interfere with your ability and capacity to function. Most of the time, a person in a hypomanic episode may not require hospitalization.

DEPRESSIVE EPISODE

Depressive episodes may be characterized by low moods, extended periods of hopelessness, loss of interest in people and activities you love, and extreme emptiness. You may feel unworthy and guilty, and even entertain suicidal thoughts and thoughts of self-harm.

MIXED EPISODE

When you are in a mixed episode, you will experience symptoms of depression and mania at the same time. These may be accompanied by aggressive behavior, and you may need to be hospitalized when it comes to this.

MANIA AND HYPOMANIA DIFFERENCES

Both mania and hypomania are characterized by mood changes that may lead to feelings of euphoria, excitement, and high energy. However, hypomania is less severe. Hypomanic episodes don't last as long as manic episodes and may cause less noticeable issues.

Energy levels

When you are in a manic episode, you may not sleep for days due to high energy levels. You may not be able to stay calm or seated for a few hours, either. But when you are in a hypomanic episode, you'll need to rest, albeit for a few hours, maybe three to five, and still be able to operate normally and even stay on top of a demanding schedule.

Self-perceptions and confidence levels

Manic episodes can lead you to life-threatening risks, but the risky behaviors associated with hypomania are usually much lower. On the contrary, during a hypomanic episode, confidence and self-image are much higher. This can easily make you persuasive and charming.

Euphoria

During a manic episode, the excitement is too extreme to be positive and may result in feelings of happiness and enthusiasm. In hypomania, the feelings of euphoria may seem like fun but in a way that leads to impulsiveness.

Delusions

During a manic episode, you may experience psychosis, which is characterized by hallucinations and delusions. In hypomania, it's unlikely to experience psychosis. Now, let's talk about the subtypes.

BIPOLAR I DISORDER

Bipolar I is the most common form of bipolar disorder and occurs more frequently than the other disorders listed. To be diagnosed with this disorder, you must have had at least a single manic episode that lasts for at least seven days.[7] You must have also had several manic episodes, and those must last longer than seven days. The manic episodes may or may not be accompanied by hypomanic episodes, depressive, and mixed states. Many bipolar I disorder patients also have neutral moods. During the manic episodes, you may feel like you are on top of the world. You may also experience great excitement and an increase in energy levels. If left untreated, the manic episode can last three to six months, while any experience of depression in between may go on for about six months to one year.

This type of bipolar disorder affects the two genders (men and women) equally.[8]

BIPOLAR II DISORDER

To be conclusively diagnosed with bipolar II disorder, you must have had at least a single major depressive episode that lasted at least two weeks, accompanied by at least a single hypomanic episode.[1] Between these episodes, you may go back to your normal routines. This means, shifting between the less severe episodes of hypomania and depression. Normally, people with bipolar II disorder don't have manic episodes, at least not noticeable ones.

People with bipolar II disorder typically seek medical help following the depressive episodes because the hypomanic episodes may feel fun and pleasurable, sometimes even boosting their general performance. When they seek medical help, bipolar II disorder could be misdiagnosed as depression. That's because the hypomanic episode that felt pleasurable was ignored, and they only went to the doctor during the depressive episode with depressive symptoms. Since people with bipolar II disorder normally don't experience manic episodes, depressive episodes become the focus of treatment.

Bipolar II disorder may also be accompanied by other mental health and psychological problems, such as substance abuse and anxiety disorders. Substance abuse disorder can aggravate symptoms of depression and mania.

So, what's the difference between bipolar I disorder and bipolar II disorder?

As previously stated, bipolar I disorder normally involves manic episodes. Sometimes, depressive episodes may also occur. Bipolar II disorder, on the contrary, involves depression and hypomania.

Which one of the two is more serious?

Well, most people assume that bipolar I disorder is more serious because it involves manic episodes, which can be intense and may require hospitalization. However, bipolar II disorder can also be just as challenging to manage and treat. Research indicates that the depressive episodes linked to bipolar II disorder occur frequently and may last longer than the manic episodes associated with bipolar I disorder. The symptoms may also persist longer in life.[5]

CYCLOTHYMIC DISORDER

A cyclothymic disorder is a less severe form of bipolar disorder characterized by frequent but less severe episodes of hypomania and depressive symptoms.[1]

The symptoms must be present for at least two years to receive a cyclothymic disorder diagnosis. The mood changes associated with cyclothymic disorder occur in cycles, coming in highs and lows. You may feel like your mood has stabilized between those highs and lows.

So, what's the difference between bipolar disorder and cyclothymic disorder?

The intensity of symptoms is what differentiates bipolar disorder from cyclothymic disorder. The symptoms associated with bipolar are more intense, most of which meet clinical criteria for the diagnosis of mania or major depression. However, the symptoms of cyclothymic disorder aren't as intense and normally don't meet the criteria for clinical diagnosis.[8] They are mild "ups and downs" with periods of normal moods as well, even though those don't last too long. Untreated, cyclothymic disorder increases your risk of developing bipolar disorder itself. The cyclothymic disorder normally starts in a person's adolescent years. During this time, you may appear to function normally; however, you may come across as "difficult" or "moody" to those around you, especially before getting diagnosed.

Sadly, most people with cyclothymic disorder don't seek treatment early on because the mood swings are mild. Sometimes, a person with cyclothymic disorder may experience periods of high productivity. The Diagnostic Manual of Mental Disorders (DSM-V), argues that cyclothymic disorder lacks the complete criteria for either of the episodes associated with bipolar disorder—mania, hypomania, major depression, and mixed states.[9] Still, people with cyclothymic disorder may develop either form of bipolar (bipolar I or bipolar II disorder) later in life, especially if they don't seek proper treatment.

MIXED BIPOLAR STATE

This is where someone experiences both mania and depression simultaneously. Mixed bipolar states are often characterized by feelings of high energy accompanied by intense feelings of hopelessness and sadness.

RAPID CYCLING BIPOLAR

If you experience four or more episodes of mania, hypomania, depression, and mixed states, in a single year, then you could be diagnosed with rapid cycling bipolar.

OTHER SPECIFIED BIPOLAR-RELATED DISORDERS

These are bipolar-like disorders that haven't met the full criteria for any of the disorders mentioned so far because they are either too mild or too short to be fully categorized. They may include:

- Major depressive episodes that are accompanied by short cycles of hypomania, for example, two or three days.
- A hypomanic episode with insufficient symptoms accompanied by major depressive episodes.
- Hypomanic episodes with no previous history of a major depressive episode.
- Short cycles of cyclothymia—less than two years.

OTHER UNSPECIFIED BIPOLAR AND RELATED DISORDERS

It's also possible to experience symptoms of bipolar and its related disorders but in a way that doesn't meet the criteria for the other mentioned disorders, fully. This type of diagnosis may be used in emergencies where there isn't enough information for a full diagnosis.

DRUG AND SUBSTANCE-INDUCED BIPOLAR AND RELATED DISORDERS

You may also experience a persistent and noticeable mood change with high emotions and irritability. This may happen with or without depression, but in a way that distinctly reduces pleasure in all activities. There must be sufficient evidence that these symptoms developed following substance use or withdrawal from substance use. The substances may be stimulants, hallucinogens, sedatives, amphetamines, and many others.[8]

BIPOLAR AND RELATED DISORDERS RESULTING FROM OTHER MEDICAL CONDITIONS

This may happen when there are symptoms of bipolar and enough evidence of a link to other medical conditions, such as hyperthyroidism, bronchitis, pulmonary embolism, and chronic obstructive pulmonary disease.[8]

CO-MORBIDITIES—OTHER MEDICAL CONDITIONS OCCURRING WITH BIPOLAR

People with bipolar disorder may also have an increased risk of developing other conditions, such as:

- Anxiety.
- Obesity.
- Suicidal thoughts.
- Self-harm.
- Cardiovascular diseases.
- Drug and alcohol abuse.
- Addictions.

When this happens, the accompanying disorder may need to be managed alongside bipolar disorder. It is important that you speak to your healthcare provider about everything you are experiencing so that nothing is missed.

BIPOLAR DISORDER LOOKS DIFFERENT FOR EVERYONE

Bipolar disorder has been described as *"the chameleon of psychiatry."*[10] Why?

Bipolar disorder is characterized by emotional extremes (highs and lows), which can also favor other mental health conditions. Because the main issue with bipolar disorder is mood regulation, it can present different symptoms at different times. For example, people affected by the classic form of bipolar disorder have periods of mania (the opposite of depression), accompanied by periods of intense, severe depression. The reality that these extremely different moods occur at different times but within the same period gave rise to the older name—manic-depressive disorder.[2]

These extreme mood changes occur simultaneously because the brain chemistry and sometimes function of a person with bipolar disorder are often altered.[11]

The mood regulation mechanisms don't work normally. This means that even two episodes may present different symptoms in the same individual.

Moreover, no two people with bipolar disorder will report the same experience—and more generally, research indicates that there are important overarching differences between how men and women experience bipolar disorder too.[8]

The symptoms of mania and depression manifest differently in everyone. They may appear and reappear over time and occur together with other illnesses. It's not surprising, then, that it sometimes takes years between the first time someone experiences an episode and when they are finally diagnosed. Because bipolar disorder is so complicated, it's very hard to pin down. Many people don't even realize they have it. Many others don't know that they need help. It's therefore important for families to pay close attention to their loved ones.

When it comes to bipolar disorder, family members should come first. They can act as thermometers because they know when one of the members isn't okay. They know when something is wrong. It's not their responsibility to diagnose each other because it takes a trained healthcare professional to do that. Still, they can encourage each other to get the proper help they need following an episode.[9]

CHAPTER 2

THE SYMPTOMS, EARLY WARNING SIGNS, AND ROOT CAUSES

B ipolar disorder is a complex and often complicated mood disorder that may result from a mix of social, environmental, biological and physical factors. For this reason, and due to the nature of the disorder, it's important to understand the medical and technical aspects. Bear with me as we dive into the details of all the medical and technical information and jargon that will help us better understand this disorder.

The National Alliance on Mental Illness, has reported that bipolar disorder varies from one person to the next. The intensity and frequency with which symptoms manifest can also vary. Depending on the person, the episodes may last several days, even up to weeks.[1] Moreover, people with bipolar disorders may also experience extended periods of calmness, where there are no episodes, and they show no symptoms.

Others may struggle more, experiencing the "highs" and "lows" quickly. We now know that when moods occur simultaneously, a person will be experiencing what's known as mixed states, and when they happen in quick succession, that's known as rapid cycling. Although bipolar disorder can start at any age, including childhood and tween years, the symptoms and diagnosis tend to appear between late teens and early to late twenties—say anywhere from the age of 18 through the age of 29. It's also possible to develop bipolar disorder much later in life, but it's highly unlikely for it to occur above age 40.[1]

EARLY WARNING SIGNS OF BIPOLAR DISORDER

When you are dealing with symptoms of bipolar disorder, your thoughts and behavior are normally beyond your control. Family and close friends might be the ones to notice the changes in behavior. An early warning symptom is hypomania, where you may feel great, impulsive, excited, and highly energetic.

Common early signs of mania and hypomania:

- Not sleeping in a manic/hypomanic episode is the most commonly experienced early sign of bipolar disorder.
- Becoming irritated and agitated.
- Displaying intense emotions.
- Suddenly becoming extremely energized with new plans, schemes, ideas, goals, and motivations.
- Having a hard time concentrating.
- Talking extremely fast. Rapid thoughts usually accompany the fast speech.
- If you have money, spending it fast and unreasonably
- Having increased paranoia and paranoid thoughts.
- Refusing to eat.
- Easily losing track of time.
- Seeing "codes." This means reading into words, patterns, and events too much.
- Becoming persuasive and insistent.
- Easily getting into arguments with family and close friends.
- Having a high drive without the desire to stop and rest, eat, or sleep.
- Having a sudden obsession with spiritual ideas and religious themes.

- Taking on more work and working extremely hard on your new projects.

Common early warning signs of depression:

- Fatigue.
- Irritability.
- Insomnia or excessive sleeping.
- Staying up too late to either work on projects, scroll on the phone, or just watch TV.
- Lack of concentration.
- Lack of motivation.
- Withdrawal—no desire for social contact, avoiding calls and texts, not attending social activities.
- Lack of appetite or overeating.
- Anxiety.
- Hopelessness and increased feelings of worthlessness.
- Complete loss of interest in things one once loved, such as hobbies and other leisure activities.
- Constantly listening to sad music.
- Taking lots of sick days.

- Extreme procrastination and staying away from responsibilities.
- Suicidal thoughts.
- Thoughts of self-harm.

If you spot one of these early warning signs of bipolar disorder, it's best to talk to a mental healthcare provider.

BIPOLAR I DISORDER – THE SYMPTOMS

Manic episode

During a manic episode (which lasts at least one week), you may feel excited and high-spirited. You may also feel irritable and show at least three of the following symptoms:

- Operating normally and feeling energetic despite receiving little to no sleep.
- Talking extremely fast.
- Developing racing thoughts that lead you to change ideas quickly and randomly.
- Becoming distracted.

- Being restless and having an increased motivation that pushes you to get started on or work on multiple projects simultaneously.
- Exhibiting risky behavior.
- Having false beliefs.
- Having disorganized thinking.
- Experiencing psychosis—delusions and hallucinations.

When you are having an acute manic episode, you may also have delusions that are irrational, illogical, false, and fixed. For example, you may hold a particular false belief and stay fixated on it such that you never give in, even after endless, repeated, and persuasive explanations that the belief isn't real. When you are acting on delusional beliefs, you may put yourself and others at risk. You may believe, for example, that you have wings and can fly and may even try jumping out of a window. This is risky behavior.

Two types of delusions can appear during a manic episode—grandiose and persecutory delusions.[2] When you are having grandiose delusions, you may believe you have extraordinary powers and access to certain beliefs and privileges. This extreme level of delusion is normally described as "mood congruent." For example, someone may believe they are a powerful king or Jesus Christ and can perform miracles, make millions of dollars, or teleport.

In persecutory delusions, you may believe that you are being followed, that some people are after you, or that something bad is about to happen to you or a loved one. Although persecutory delusions may be part of mania, they are also present in other psychotic illnesses and, therefore, should not lead to a conclusive diagnosis of bipolar disorder on their own.

With hallucinations—you may hear, see, and sense things that aren't real. Psychotic symptoms don't manifest in hypomania (bipolar II disorder), and this is one of the most distinctive features of bipolar I disorder. The most common hallucination that may happen in mania is hearing things, also known as auditory hallucinations. You may hear footsteps approaching, a familiar or unfamiliar voice(s) that can either be male or female, and a voice or voices calling out your name. They may tell you to do things and comment about what you are doing. When there are multiple voices, you may hear them talking about you. You may hear voices that sound like they are coming from outside your head, when in reality, you are only hearing your own thoughts, and the voice(s) are normally only in your head.

With visual hallucinations—you may see things that don't exist. The visual hallucinations can be complex, too, leading you to see whole scenes. Visual hallucinations are uncommon with manic episodes but often occur when there are other complex physical and organic complications.

Hypomanic episode

Hypomanic episodes are usually characterized by the same symptoms observed in mania but less severe. The symptoms last around 4 days, unlike in mania, where symptoms should last at least one week. The symptoms may include:

- Operating normally and feeling energetic despite receiving little to no sleep.
- Talking extremely fast.
- Developing racing thoughts that may lead you to change ideas quickly and randomly.
- Becoming easily distracted.
- Being restless and having an increased motivation that pushes you to get started

on or work on multiple projects
simultaneously.

- Exhibiting risky behavior.

Depressive episode

A bipolar I disorder-related depressive episode
must last at least two weeks, and one must show at
least five of the symptoms described below:

- Feeling hopeless and in despair.
- Having intense sadness.
- Completely losing interest in activities that
  were once enjoyed.
- Being fatigued.
- Developing strong feelings of guilt and
  worthlessness.
- Getting more or less sleep.
- Having a lack of or increased appetite.
- Having slowed movement and speech.
- Being restless.
- Having difficulty concentrating.
- Low self-esteem.
- Suicidal thoughts.
- Thoughts of death and self-harm.

BIPOLAR II DISORDER – THE SYMPTOMS

Hypomanic episode

Hypomanic episodes may make you quite pleasant and fun to be around. While in a hypomanic episode, you may make jokes, take an interest in other people's lives and activities, appear like the "life of the party," and positively influence people around you. Maybe you are wondering, *"What is so bad about that?"*

Hypomania is often accompanied by erratic and unhealthy behavior as well. Moreover, hypomania can spiral into full mania to the degree that it negatively impacts your ability to function normally. You may also find yourself:

- Showcasing euphoria and feelings of excitement.
- Quickly switching from one idea to another.
- Having increased self-confidence.
- Exhibiting loud, rapid, and uninterruptible speech.
- Becoming hyperactive.
- Operating on less sleep.

- Having high energy.

Depressive episode

The depressive episodes associated with bipolar II disorder resemble the normal clinical depression with symptoms including:

- Having a loss of pleasure.
- Feelings of worthlessness.
- Guilt.
- Hopelessness.
- Suicidal thoughts.
- Loss of energy.
- Fatigue, among other things.

A majority of people with bipolar II disorder have more depressive episodes compared to hypomanic episodes. The chances of developing depression are also increased following a hypomanic episode. Many people with bipolar II disorder cycle back and forth between hypomanic episodes and depression, while others have long periods of calm between those episodes. Untreated hypomania can go on for months. Most of the time, symptoms will last a few weeks to a few months.

CYCLOTHYMIC DISORDER – THE SYMPTOMS

In cyclothymic disorder, you may experience multiple hypomanic symptoms, although those symptoms don't normally meet the criteria for either a bipolar I or bipolar II disorder diagnosis. The symptoms are generally mild compared to those of either bipolar I or bipolar II.

THE ROOT CAUSES OF BIPOLAR DISORDER

No one understands or knows exactly what causes bipolar disorder. Lots of studies have been done on possible causes, and researchers often conclude that there may be a combination of genetic components, social conditions, and environmental factors that could lead to bipolar disorder.

Genetic factors

Research shows a genetic component linked to bipolar disorder. When discussing genetic factors, the most important question becomes, can bipolar disorder be inherited? The answer is—yes, it is possible. Bipolar disorder can be passed down genetically.[2] This isn't to say that there is a "bipolar gene" that you can inherit. No, but family links are quite complex. If you have bipolar disorder, there's a high chance one of your family members also experiences bipolar-related mood episodes. They may or may not have a formal diagnosis yet. The genetic component linked to bipolar disorder has been studied widely through different family structures, including twins, adopted children, and multiple families.[1]

For example, in a family, first-degree relatives such as siblings and the children, have an increased chance of developing a mood disorder if someone in that family tree has already been diagnosed with bipolar disorder. Suppose one parent has bipolar disorder, in that case, there will be a 10% chance that their offspring develops bipolar disorder as well. If both parents have bipolar disorder, then the likelihood that their child develops bipolar disorder rises by up to 40%.[1]

In the case of twins—research shows that if an identical twin has bipolar disorder, there will be a 40-70% chance that the other twin will have it as well. If the twins are fraternal, then there is a 5-10% chance that both will have bipolar disorder.[2]

These are critical findings, particularly in the argument that genetics do play a role in bipolar disorder. After all, identical twins are born when a single fertilized egg splits, meaning the two babies have the same genetic material.

However, these findings do not automatically mean that if there's a family history of bipolar disorder, then other family members will develop it as well. Still, the chances of having this mood disorder are much lower in families where there is no bipolar disorder recognized.

Brain structure

When trying to understand exactly what it is about the brain that is inherited, neurotransmitters have received a great deal of attention. But what are neurotransmitters? They are chemical messengers being sent back and forth throughout the body.[3] They carry and boost messages from the brain to different body parts such as glands, muscles, etc. If you want to pick up a mug of coffee, for example, neurons carry this message from the brain to your hand muscles so you can pick the mug up.

There are billions of neurons working at any one time, sending hundreds of billions of messages to different parts of the body.[3] These neurons control your heart rate, digestion, learning, and concentration levels. Neurons also control your psychological functions, including joy, fear, anger, etc.

Our bodies have four types of neurotransmitters—dopamine, glutamate, serotonin, and acetylcholine. Once there is an imbalance of a single neurotransmitter (too high or too low), then mood disorders can occur.[3]

Other studies indicate that an imbalance of the four neurotransmitters could be the problem. This is to say that maybe a particular neurotransmitter level isn't as important as its level in relation to the other three. If, for example, three neurotransmitters are at 100% and one is at 90%, a mood disorder could occur. Still, others believe that a change in the sensitivity of these receptors could be the problem.[3]

What's more, there is enough proof showing that certain psychiatric medications can treat bipolar. Most of those medications target neurotransmitters—our brain's chemical messengers. This indicates that bipolar disorder may be linked to certain functional problems associated with these chemical messengers.[3] While many believe this is true, no one truly understands how this works. Moreover, no one can definitely say that neurotransmitters are indeed the cause or result of bipolar disorder.

Societal influences and stressful life events

Mood disorders normally and frequently start spontaneously, but stressful life events and circumstances can also trigger them. You may be able to link the onset of your mood symptoms to certain stressful experiences in your life. Again, stress may aggravate the symptoms of a mood disorder, so they are more intense or harder to manage.

No one understands the exact way these stressful events trigger bipolar disorder, but experts believe that the stress hormone known as cortisol could be a culprit. Stress leads to increased cortisol production, which may cause brain function and communication changes. Research has shown that the levels of cortisol often stay high in people with depression or bipolar disorder even when they aren't stressed or in a mood episode.[4] Life events that can cause stress include:

- Loss of a loved one—family member, a friend, a pet, etc.
- Poverty and financial worries.
- Trauma in any form.
- Abuse, bullying, and harassment.
- Loneliness and isolation.

- Change and uncertainty.
- The pressure of work or study.
- Big events such as weddings, birth of a child, holidays, etc.

Please understand that there is no one specific way to define stress. It can happen for different reasons, and it affects everyone differently. What I may find stressful, another person going through the same thing may not perceive as stressful.

Environmental triggers

Once someone has been diagnosed with bipolar disorder, small environmental stressors may lead to intense mood changes. For example:

- Lack of sleep or sleep disruption.
- Stressful life events.
- Stress in general.
- Illness.
- Physical injury.
- Lack of exercise.
- Menstruation.
- Loud music and noises.
- Falling in love.

- Vacations.
- Late-night parties.
- When starting/working on creative projects.

Childhood trauma

Some people believe that emotional distress during a child's developmental years can lead to bipolar disorder later in life. That's because childhood trauma that leads to intense emotional distress can impair a person's ability to deal with and manage their emotions. This may be due to experiences such as:

- Neglect.
- Emotional abuse.
- Physical or sexual abuse.
- Traumatic events—such as the loss of a close and beloved family member like a parent, grandparent, or an adored pet.

Medication and substance abuse

Yes, certain medications and drugs may trigger bipolar moods and symptoms. Some medications have been linked to mania and hypomania as a side effect. This could happen while you are in the process of taking the medication or when you stop taking it as a form of withdrawal. This may include medication prescribed for both psychiatric and physical illnesses, including antidepressants.[4]

Moreover, depression may also be a side effect of taking a lot of different medicines. Possible side effects of a particular medication should be an important subject of discussion with your doctor.

Recreational drugs

Recreational drugs can also lead to mania, depression, or hypomania. Always talk to your doctor if you are worried about the side effects of a particular medicine or a recreational drug.[4]

Common relapse triggers

- Recreational drugs.
- Alcohol consumption.
- Negative and stressful life events.
- Changes in sleep patterns—too little or too much sleep.

- Metabolic stress from irregular eating and sleeping patterns or irregular physical activity.
- Flying abroad.
- Too much caffeine that could interfere with sleep patterns.
- Stopping prescribed medication without proper consultation.
- Disruption of sleep-wake patterns.

GETTING THE RIGHT DIAGNOSIS

Getting the right diagnosis for bipolar disorder isn't as simple as sending blood to the lab and waiting for results to come back after a while. Yes, bipolar disorder has a distinctive set of symptoms, but there's no single known test that can be used to confirm it conclusively.[5] Often, a doctor must employ a combination of different methods to develop a final diagnosis. Bipolar disorder is often characterized by intense mood episodes that occur differently with every patient. How people experience the different symptoms will vary from person to person.

To get the right diagnosis, you must talk to a healthcare professional. The healthcare professional will do a physical exam, after which they'll ask about your family and medical history. They'll also ask about your life experiences and the symptoms you've experienced thus far. Suppose your healthcare provider believes you could have bipolar disorder; they will quickly refer you to a psychiatrist. The psychiatrist will then do a detailed mental health evaluation.

The healthcare provider may ask you the following questions:

- What symptoms you experienced, and how many there were?
- If you ever experienced a mood episode, and which types they were?
- How long did those episodes last?
- How many episodes have you had so far?
- How have your symptoms affected your life so far?
- What your family history was, and was there anyone with similar symptoms or diagnosis in your family?
- What thoughts and feelings you had during specific episodes?
- Did you feel like you were in control of

your episodes, or were they out of your
control?

- When did you first start to experience your
  symptoms?
- Have you ever had suicidal thoughts or
  feelings of self-harm?
- Have you had a history of drug/substance
  abuse?

The healthcare provider may also:

- Ask your permission to talk to your loved
  ones about your behavior to understand
  your symptoms better.
- Request you to keep a journal and record
  your moods so you can see possible
  triggers and patterns.
- Do a physical health examination. For
  example, certain thyroid issues can lead to
  mania-like symptoms.

The diagnosis must also consider medications
you've taken in the past and your medical history.

How long does a diagnosis take?

We already know that bipolar disorder involves mood changes. These changes happen over time, so the healthcare provider may need to observe you for a while before coming up with a conclusive diagnosis. The healthcare provider must be extremely careful to give you the right diagnosis. As it is, the symptoms of bipolar disorder are known to overlap with other disorders. For this reason, those symptoms can easily be confused with other mental health conditions, particularly in the early stages, which is normally in the teenage years.

The sadness that manifests as a result of an episode may resemble major depression. The excitement, energy, and even irritability seen in some episodes may resemble the symptoms of Attention Deficit Hyperactive Disorder (ADHD). Other symptoms may also resemble those found in borderline personality disorders, schizophrenia, post-traumatic stress disorders, conduct disorders, anxiety disorders, obsessive-compulsive disorders, personality disorders, and schizoaffective disorders.[6] Because of these complexities, you may go weeks, months, or even years before you finally get a diagnosis.

Other factors that lead to a misdiagnosis include inconsistencies in mood changes and the timeline of the episodes. What's more, most people don't seek treatment unless they encounter a depressive episode. No one runs to a doctor to tell them they are excited, extremely happy, and so energetic they feel like they can conquer the world.

There are still no specific blood tests that can be done to help diagnose bipolar disorder. No brain scans can be done to help diagnose bipolar disorder, either. Even then, the healthcare provider will have to do a physical exam and other lab tests, such as urine and thyroid analysis, to rule out the possibility of other conditions. Even when that diagnosis has been made, it may not always be right. Healthcare providers don't always get it right. Reports show that there is a 76.8% rate of misdiagnosis linked to bipolar disorder.[6] This means there is a high chance the patient will get a wrong diagnosis. For this reason, you may:

- Not get a bipolar diagnosis even when you feel like you should get it.
- You may get a diagnosis for a mental health problem you didn't expect and may not agree with it.
- Get a diagnosis, but still think it's incorrect.
- You may think your diagnosis is correct

but still feel like it doesn't go hand in hand with your symptoms.

Talk to your doctor if you have doubts or are unhappy about your diagnosis. You have a voice, and it's your responsibility to ensure it is heard. More importantly, try to get a second opinion from another expert if you are unhappy with your diagnosis.

After a diagnosis, you may deal with a wide range of emotions, especially when the reality that bipolar disorder is a life-long condition starts to sink. Some people react with the following.

Denial or complete disbelief

Any diagnosis can be difficult to deal with. When you finally get a bipolar disorder diagnosis, you may be in complete disbelief or deny it altogether. Many people will start looking for another explanation that makes sense to them. Others will ignore it completely.

Hope and relief at finally learning what it is

Now, your struggles make sense, and there's new hope for getting the medication and help you need. This can bring a lot of relief.

Anger and grief

Some people may feel upset about their bipolar disorder diagnosis, which often stems from fear and worry about what the future holds. You may worry about the loss of your "normal" life as you knew it before the diagnosis.

Taking action immediately

Once you receive your diagnosis, you may jump into action immediately. You may start reading about bipolar disorder, its causes, types, treatment options, and how to manage it. While this reaction can be good, you'll have to slow down at some point, let the news sink in, and then deal with any emotions that arise.

Blame

Some people may want to blame someone else for this outcome. You may want this to be someone else's fault because if you believe it is, you may also think there is a way to change it. But you shouldn't lose hope because when managed right, you can lead a healthy, happy life and maybe someday grow out and be healed from this disorder. Indeed, bipolar disorder was traditionally thought to be a life-long disorder, but new research indicates that up to 50% of patients diagnosed between ages 18 and 25 could outgrow the illness by the time they reach the age of 30.[6]

As harsh as these reactions may seem, they are completely normal. They are also quite common but usually not helpful. The best way to deal with the new diagnosis is to get the correct information and get started on the right treatment plan as soon as possible.

How to tell if you've been misdiagnosed

It's not an easy task to tell whether you've been misdiagnosed or the disorder has been missed. However, there may be signs that you have been misdiagnosed. These are including:

- Being on a treatment plan but making little to no progress with it. Said differently, the current medication or therapy option isn't working.
- Being on a treatment plan, but your symptoms have worsened.

- Having symptoms that don't fit your current diagnosis.
- You've been given a diagnosis, but your symptoms are far from the normal symptoms of that diagnosis.

If you believe you've been misdiagnosed, speak with your healthcare provider. If necessary, get a second opinion from another doctor.

Is it necessary to get a second opinion?

It doesn't hurt to get someone else to confirm your diagnosis, but if you are working with a trustworthy healthcare provider who has taken the time to do all necessary tests and think they are right, you don't need a second opinion. Still, you can advocate for a second opinion if you feel like you've been misdiagnosed. As I mentioned before, the good news is that while bipolar disorder was traditionally thought to be a lifelong disorder, new research indicates that up to 50% of patients diagnosed between ages 18 and 25 could outgrow the illness by the time they reach the age of 30.[6]

CHAPTER 3

THE EFFECTS OF BIPOLAR DISORDER

I magine living your life on a rollercoaster where you have zero to no control over the ride's speed, direction, or intensity. This is how countless teens live. Living with bipolar disorder, which is often characterized by extreme shifts in moods, energy levels, and behavior, can make it hard to navigate through your daily life. One moment, you are soaring at the exhilarating highs of mania, having great energy and ideas. The next moment, you are crushing into the depths of depression, battling overwhelming sadness and negative emotions.

Bipolar disorder introduces a dynamic interplay of moods, challenging the traditional ways of adolescence. It's not just about the extremes of highs and lows but the subtle shadows that color every relationship, every decision, every interaction, and every moment. From emotional regulation and relationships to school performance and substance use, we will spend the next few moments discussing the different challenges you face as a teenager dealing with this order.

MOOD REGULATION

Bipolar disorder is primarily recognized as a mood issue, which, in turn, affects daily life functioning. When you have this condition, you get to experience two distinct emotional states: manic episodes and depressive episodes. Manic episodes are characterized by heightened energy, talkativeness, euphoria, and impulsivity. In contrast, depressive episodes are marked by a lack of interest in previously enjoyed life activities, lethargy, profound sadness, lack of energy, and inability to focus. Simple daily tasks like preparing meals, getting out of bed, or going to school often feel tiring and exhausting.

These mood fluctuations disrupt daily life activities such as academic performance, relationships, and self-care routines, which make it difficult to maintain consistency and stability in emotions and behaviors. The unpredictability of mood swings makes it impossible to tell the frequency or the intensity of the episodes; living with this condition means you could go to sleep in a depressive episode and wake up at the onset of a maniac state with little to no control over these emotions. It affects relationships and social interactions because, most of the time, family members, friends, and schoolmates find it difficult to comprehend the sudden fluctuations in moods and behavior, leading to strained relationships and feelings of isolation. Maintaining balance in commitments and routines also becomes difficult as you cannot tell how you will feel from one moment to the next.

As a result, this leads to missing out on life experiences because living with bipolar disorder leads to avoiding social interactions out of the fear of being unable to cope with the mood shifts. Being unable to perform daily tasks as a teenager who suffers from such a disorder, may not align with the normal life experiences that others effortlessly have, which can lead to feelings of frustration and loneliness, further complicating the efforts of mood regulations.

RELATIONSHIPS

Bipolar disorder can significantly impact relationships in teenagers, adding a new layer of complexity to their interactions with friends, family, and peers. The nature of bipolar disorder, characterized by extreme mood swings between mania and depression, can influence various aspects of interpersonal connections. Here are some ways in which bipolar disorder might affect relationships in teenagers.

Intense mood swings

The most distinguishing feature of bipolar disorder is the presence of intense mood swings. During manic phases, teenagers may display high energy, creativity, and impulsivity levels. This can make relationships exhilarating, but challenging to keep up with. Conversely, during depressive episodes, they may withdraw, become irritable, or lose interest in socializing, affecting the depth and quality of connections.

Self-stigma

Also known as internalized sigma, this is one of the major things that makes it challenging for teenagers to establish healthy relationships, which can result in self-created solitude. Self-stigma happens when someone internalizes what people say about those who have mental health conditions. The negative messages that spread about mental health conditions make people suffering from these conditions feel bad about themselves, and in return, develop low self-esteem. Establishing or initiating a relationship becomes difficult when you are self-conscious. With bipolar disorder, it feels safe to push people away when you have feelings of not being good enough.

Struggles with communication

Effective and clear communication is vital in any relationship, but bipolar disorder can make that difficult. The most crucial part of building and maintaining a relationship is consistent communication and willingness to make an effort. Teenagers may struggle to express their needs or explain their mood shifts to friends and family. Misunderstandings can arise when those close to you need help interpreting or responding to the rapid emotional shifts they see and try to understand.

Impact on friendships

Maintaining friendships can be a rollercoaster for teenagers with bipolar disorder. Friends may find it challenging to keep up with the unpredictable changes in the various moods and behaviors exhibited. During manic phases, the individual might be the life of the party, while in depressive phases, they may withdraw, making it tough for friends to offer the support needed.

Family dynamics

The impact on family relationships can be profound. Parents may struggle to understand and navigate the highs and lows, often feeling helpless. Siblings may experience frustration or confusion as they witness the emotional turbulence within the family. Balancing support with the need for independence becomes a delicate task.

Risk of impulsivity

During manic phases, teenagers with bipolar disorder may engage in impulsive behaviors that can strain relationships. This could include risky activities, excessive spending, or decisions that affect others without considering the consequences. These actions may lead to conflict and strain on relationships. During depressive episodes, teenagers with bipolar disorder may feel low, suicidal, hopeless, and unwilling to participate in activities they once enjoyed. This could put a big strain on their relationships, as friends and family struggle to understand and keep up with their low moods.

Stigma and understanding

The stigma surrounding mental health and its surrounding conditions, like bipolar disorder, can affect social relationships, especially during adolescent years when social interactions and peer relationships are essential for emotional growth. Teenagers with this condition may face judgment or misunderstanding from peers, making them feel isolated and lonely, which in turn makes it challenging to establish and maintain healthy connections. Increasing awareness and understanding among friends and family can help reduce stigma and foster supportive environments.

Treatment compliance

The challenges of managing bipolar disorder often involve adherence to a treatment plan, which may include medication and therapy. Encouraging teenagers to follow their treatment plan can be a shared responsibility among family and friends, as it plays a crucial part in stabilizing mood swings and maintaining healthy relationships. You can build meaningful and fulfilling relationships and connections when you know you will get the support, understanding, and treatment needed.[1]

Open communication, awareness about the condition, and a supportive network are essential components in navigating the challenges posed by bipolar disorder in the world of relationships.

WORK AND YOUR FUTURE

Bipolar disorder can have significant implications for a teenager's work and prospects, introducing challenges that extend beyond the realm of personal relationships. The condition's impact on mood stability and daily functioning can influence academic performance, career choices, and long-term aspirations. Here are some ways in which bipolar disorder may affect work and plans for teenagers.

Academic performance

Bipolar disorder can disrupt a teenager's academic

journey, affecting their ability to meet educational
expectations consistently. The fluctuating energy
levels and mood changes may lead to periods of high
productivity, followed by decreased motivation and
focus. This inconsistency can impact grades and
potentially influence a teenager's pursuit of higher
education and future career paths.

Career choices

The unpredictable nature of bipolar disorder may
pose challenges when it comes to making career decisions. Teenagers with bipolar disorder may struggle to
envision a stable and sustainable career path, as
concerns about managing the condition's impact on
work performance and relationships with colleagues
may come into play. The fear of instability can affect
their confidence in pursuing certain professions.

Workplace relationships

Maintaining stable relationships with colleagues
and supervisors can be challenging for those
entering the workforce. The mood swings linked to
bipolar disorder may affect interpersonal dynamics,
making it crucial for teenagers to develop coping

strategies and communication skills. Open dialogue about the condition with employers may become necessary to foster understanding and support in the workplace.

Consistency and routine

Bipolar disorder can disrupt the consistency and routine required for success in many professions. The need for stability in work schedules, deadlines, and responsibilities may clash with the unpredictable nature of the condition. Establishing a balance between the demands of a job and the need for flexibility can become an ongoing challenge for teenagers managing bipolar disorder.

Future planning

Planning for the future, such as setting long-term goals or envisioning a career trajectory, can be complicated by the uncertainty associated with bipolar disorder. The condition may need to be clarified about the feasibility of achieving certain aspirations, which may lead to reevaluating plans. Teens may need additional support and guidance in setting realistic and adaptable goals.

Seeking professional help

Accessing mental health support becomes crucial for teenagers with bipolar disorder as they navigate the challenges of work and future planning. Incorporating therapy, medication, and coping mechanisms into the daily routine can enhance their ability to manage the condition effectively, reducing the impact on their professional and personal lives.[1]

Despite these challenges, it's important to note that with the right support, treatment, and coping strategies, teenagers with bipolar disorder can still pursue fulfilling careers and achieve their aspirations. Open communication about your condition, the development of effective coping mechanisms, and a supportive network can play pivotal roles in helping you navigate the complexities of work and future planning while managing this disorder.[1]

HOBBIES

As a teenager with bipolar disorder, you might often experience notable shifts in your interest and engagement with hobbies, particularly during manic and depressive episodes. During a manic episode, you may exhibit a sudden and intense interest in various hobbies. This heightened enthusiasm can be characterized by an influx of creative energy, which may lead you to explore and immerse yourself in different activities. Hobbies may become a means of channeling the heightened energy levels and creativity associated with mania. But during a depressive episode, you may lose interest in the things you once loved and avoid them, choosing to withdraw from people, hobbies, and other activities instead.

Bipolar disorder can significantly influence the pursuit and enjoyment of hobbies for you, introducing both challenges and opportunities for personal expression. The impact of bipolar disorder on hobbies can vary, affecting the level of engagement, consistency, and overall experience of these activities. Here are some ways in which bipolar disorder may influence your hobbies.

Fluctuating interest levels

You may experience fluctuations in interest and enthusiasm for your hobbies. During manic phases, you might dive into hobbies with intense passion, dedicating extensive time and energy to creative pursuits. However, during depressive episodes, the same hobbies may lose their appeal, and you may struggle to find motivation or interest.

Creativity bursts

Manic phases associated with bipolar disorder can be accompanied by bursts of creativity. You may find yourself deeply immersed in artistic or intellectual hobbies, even producing impressive work during these periods. These episodes can be characterized by heightened inspiration, which may lead to unique and innovative contributions to their chosen activities. During a depressive episode, you may struggle with inspiration and motivation. You may find yourself consumed with negative thoughts, losing interest in your work and hobbies.

Inconsistent engagement

Maintaining consistent engagement in hobbies may prove challenging when you have bipolar disorder. The energy fluctuations associated with the disorder can impact the ability to sustain interest and commitment over time. This inconsistency might lead to cycles of intense involvement followed by periods of disinterest or neglect.

Potential for obsessive hobbies

Manic phases may also contribute to developing obsessive interests or hobbies. You might become intensely focused on a particular activity, dedicating excessive time and resources to it. While this intense focus can lead to notable achievements, it may also pose challenges if it interferes with other aspects of your life. During a depressive episode, you may have less focus even in things you were once passionate about, spending less and less time on them.

Impact on social hobbies

Bipolar disorder can influence social hobbies and activities. During manic phases, you may be more outgoing, seek social interactions, and participate enthusiastically in group hobbies. In contrast, depressive episodes might lead you to withdrawal, making it challenging to maintain social connections through shared activities.

Role in coping mechanisms

Hobbies can serve as essential coping mechanisms for teenagers with bipolar disorder.

Engaging in creative or physical activities may offer a therapeutic outlet, helping you manage stress, express emotions, and regulate your mood. Hobbies can play a vital role in promoting overall well-being and providing a constructive way to navigate the challenges of bipolar disorder.

Opportunities for self-expression

Despite the challenges, hobbies can provide you with valuable opportunities for self-expression. Creative outlets, such as art, painting, writing, or music, can become powerful tools for communicating and processing emotions. Hobbies allow you to express your unique perspectives and navigate your internal experiences.

In navigating the impact of bipolar disorder on hobbies, you must recognize and adapt to your changing needs. Seeking a balance between periods of intense involvement and self-care during less motivated phases can contribute to a more sustainable and enjoyable experience with hobbies. Additionally, maintaining open communication with supportive friends, family, mental health professionals, and caregivers can provide valuable insights and assistance in finding adaptive strategies to integrate hobbies into your life.

SLEEP

Bipolar disorder can profoundly impact the establishment of a healthy sleep pattern, presenting challenges that vary across manic and depressive episodes. The extreme mood swings inherent in bipolar disorder contribute to disruptions in the natural sleep-wake cycle, which can complicate your desire to maintain a consistent and refreshing sleep routine.

Manic episodes and the reduced need for sleep

During manic episodes, you may experience a reduced need for sleep. The heightened energy levels, increased impulsivity, and racing thoughts characteristic of mania can lead to a diminished desire for sleep, or in some cases, a complete disregard for the necessity of rest. You may engage in various activities, feel invigorated despite minimal sleep, and contribute to a cycle of prolonged wakefulness.

Insomnia and hypersomnia during depressive episodes

Conversely, depressive episodes in bipolar disorder can manifest as disruptions in sleep, characterized by insomnia or hypersomnia. Insomnia involves difficulty falling or staying asleep, which may lead to reduced sleep duration. You may lie awake at night, grappling with racing thoughts or pervasive feelings of sadness. On the other hand, hypersomnia entails excessive sleepiness, where you may find yourself sleeping for extended periods yet still experiencing feelings of fatigue upon waking.

The irregularities in sleep patterns during both manic and depressive episodes can have far-reaching consequences on daily functioning. The lack of adequate sleep may result in cognitive impairments, difficulties with concentration, memory issues, and an overall impact on mood and emotional well-being. Furthermore, the fluctuations between reduced and increased sleep needs, contribute to challenges in establishing a consistent sleep routine, hindering the development of healthy sleep habits.[2]

Managing sleep disturbances is a crucial aspect of the overall treatment plan for bipolar disorder. Implementing strategies to promote good sleep, such as maintaining a regular night schedule, creating a comfortable sleep environment, and avoiding stimulants before bedtime, can contribute to better sleep quality. Additionally, you are encouraged to communicate openly with healthcare professionals about changes in sleep patterns, as this information is essential for tailoring effective interventions and ensuring a comprehensive approach to managing bipolar disorder. You can work towards creating a reasonable, balanced, and refreshing sleep pattern through a combination of therapeutic strategies, medications, and lifestyle adjustments, to enhance your overall well-being.

EATING

Bipolar disorder can have a big effect on eating habits and behaviors, introducing challenges related to appetite, weight fluctuations, and overall nutritional well-being. The influence of bipolar disorder on eating patterns can vary between manic and depressive episodes, contributing to both overeating and undereating behaviors. Here are some ways in which bipolar disorder may affect eating habits in teenagers.

Changes in appetite during manic episodes

During manic episodes, you may experience changes in appetite. Some teenagers may engage in overeating, often driven by increased energy levels, impulsivity, and a decreased need for sleep. The heightened activity associated with mania may lead to excessive food consumption, often with a preference for high-energy, sugary, or indulgent snacks. This can result in extreme weight gain and potential health concerns.[3]

Undereating or loss of appetite during depressive episodes

Conversely, depressive episodes in bipolar disorder may lead to undereating or a loss of appetite. Feelings of sadness, low energy, and decreased motivation can diminish interest in food. Teenagers may neglect regular meals and experience weight loss and nutritional deficiencies. A lack of appetite during depressive phases may contribute to a cycle of physical and emotional fatigue.[3]

Impact on body weight and nutritional health

The fluctuation between overeating and undereating during different phases of bipolar disorder can contribute to significant weight fluctuations. These weight changes may have implications for overall health, potentially leading to the development of eating disorders, nutritional deficiencies, or other health-related concerns. The impact of bipolar disorder on eating habits can also influence body image and self-esteem.

Emotional eating and coping mechanisms

Bipolar disorder may lead some teenagers to turn to food as a coping strategy, believing it could help them manage intense emotions during both manic and depressive episodes. Emotional eating, whether to soothe heightened emotions or to find comfort during low moods, can become a maladaptive coping strategy that affects overall eating patterns.

Medication side effects

Certain medications prescribed for the management of bipolar disorder may also influence appetite and eating habits. Some medications can lead to increased appetite and weight gain, while others may cause a loss of appetite. Understanding the possible side effects of drugs is crucial in addressing and managing changes in eating behaviors.[3]

Importance of monitoring and support

Given the potential impact of bipolar disorder on eating habits, you may need to receive regular monitoring and support. Healthcare providers can help by working closely with individuals to create strategies for maintaining a balanced and nutritious diet, managing weight fluctuations, and addressing emotional or behavioral eating-related challenges.

Addressing the complex relationship between bipolar disorder and eating habits in teenagers involves a multidimensional approach. This may include therapeutic interventions, nutritional counseling, medication and therapy management, and ongoing support from mental health professionals, family members, and other healthcare team members. Open communication and a comprehensive treatment plan are vital in promoting a healthy relationship with food and overall well-being for teenagers with bipolar disorder.[4]

DRUG AND ALCOHOL USE

When you are struggling with bipolar disorder, you face unique challenges when it comes to drug and alcohol use. The use of mood-altering substances like drugs and alcohol can significantly affect your mood and potentially trigger manic or depressive episodes. It's essential to understand the nuances of this relationship, recognizing that the effects can be different from person to person.

Self-medication

When you suffer from bipolar disorder, you may be tempted to use drugs or alcohol as a form of self-medication. This could be an attempt to alleviate the intense mood swings associated with the disorder.

Mood triggers

Drugs and alcohol have the potential to act as triggers for both manic and depressive episodes.[3] The impact can be unpredictable, with substances exacerbating mood swings and intensifying the emotional turmoil experienced when you have bipolar disorder.

Impulsivity and risk-taking

As a teenager, you are already more prone to impulsivity. When combined with bipolar disorder and substance use, this impulsivity can lead to heightened risk-taking behaviors, further complicating the management of the condition.

Impact on treatment

Substance use can interfere with the effectiveness of prescribed medications for bipolar disorder. This interference hinders the management of symptoms and poses additional risks to your overall well-being.

Family dynamics

The environment within the family plays a crucial role in shaping a teenager's approach to substance use. A supportive family system can mitigate the risk, while a history of substance use within the family may contribute to a higher likelihood of experimentation.

Understanding the challenging relationship between bipolar disorder and drug/alcohol use is important for both you and your support networks. This awareness lays the foundation for targeted interventions, prevention strategies, and the development of coping mechanisms that promote your well-being, while navigating the complexities of bipolar disorder.

PHYSICAL ACTIVITY

Bipolar disorder, being a complicated mood disorder, can significantly impact your physical activity levels. This is due to the disorder's hallmark mood swings, which encompass manic (or hypomanic) and depressive phases.

Manic episodes

Increased energy
Manic episodes are characterized by abnormally elevated energy levels. You may demonstrate restlessness or engage in excessive, unplanned activity.

Impulsivity
Increased impulsivity could contribute to risky choices related to physical activities, leading to a greater potential for injury.

Disrupted sleep
Sleep disturbances during manic phases can exacerbate physical health problems and affect recovery from exercise.

Depressive episodes

Reduced energy and motivation

During depressive phases, you may experience fatigue, low energy levels, stress, and a lack of motivation to engage in physical activity.

Psychomotor changes

You may experience psychomotor retardation, a slowing down of physical movements and reactions, making physical activity difficult.[5]

Loss of pleasure

Once enjoyable, activities, including sports or exercise, can lose their appeal.

Sleep disturbances

Irregular sleep patterns caused by depression can further worsen fatigue.

ACADEMIC PERFORMANCE

Bipolar disorder can significantly impact academic performance due to its effects on mood, energy levels, and overall functioning. The challenges associated with bipolar disorder may manifest in various ways, affecting different or even all aspects of your academic life. Here are some different ways in which bipolar disorder can influence academic performance.

Mood swings

Manic episodes

During manic episodes, you may experience heightened energy levels, impulsivity, distractibility, and a reduced need for sleep. While this can lead to bursts of creativity, it may also result in difficulty focusing on academic tasks, impulsively taking on too many projects, or engaging in risky behavior that affects school performance.

Depressive episodes

Depressive episodes are characterized by low emotions, energy, feelings of sadness, and difficulty concentrating. You may struggle with motivation, find it challenging to complete assignments, and experience declining academic performance.

Impaired concentration and cognitive function

Attention difficulties

Both manic and depressive phases can disrupt concentration and attention, making it difficult for you to stay focused on your studies.[6]

Memory issues

Cognitive functions such as memory, thinking, and information processing may be affected, impacting your ability to retain and recall information necessary for academic success.[6]

Impulsivity

Risky behavior

Impulsivity during manic episodes may lead to risky behaviors that can interfere with academic responsibilities, such as skipping classes, neglecting assignments, or making impulsive decisions that have academic consequences.

Inconsistent performance

Fluctuating energy levels

The unpredictable nature of this disorder can lead to inconsistent academic performance. As a teenager, you may excel during periods of elevated moods (manic phase), but struggle when experiencing a depressive episode.

Interference with social interactions

Isolation

Bipolar disorder can lead to social withdrawal during depressive episodes, affecting your ability to collaborate on group projects, participate in class discussions, or seek academic support from peers.

Treatment side effects

Medication effects

Some medications used to manage bipolar disorder may have side effects that impact cognitive function, concentration, or alertness, which can potentially influence academic performance.[3]

Attendance issues

Absenteeism

The challenges associated with bipolar disorder, especially during depressive episodes, may result in absenteeism or skipping school, affecting the continuity of learning and the ability to keep up with school work.

Bipolar disorder can have a huge impact on and disrupt a person's daily life. Still, the different and accompanying effects vary between individuals. But with appropriate treatment, many people diagnosed with bipolar go on to live full, productive and happy lives. To do this effectively, you must first learn to identify and challenge your personal behaviors. How can you do this? Let's talk about that in Chapter 4.

CHAPTER 4
CHALLENGING YOUR PERSONAL BEHAVIORS

B ehaviors can be challenging when they are intense and threaten your quality of life and physical safety. Challenging behaviors are not disabilities, but most of the time, people with a disability or mental condition are more likely to show challenging behaviors. As a teenager, you may exhibit a range of challenging behaviors as you navigate the complexities of adolescence and strive for independence. Various factors can influence these behaviors, including hormonal changes, brain development, peer influences, and family dynamics.

Some challenging personal behaviors commonly observed in teenagers, such as talking back, arguing, and lying may seem small, but they can lead to worse troubles such as drug abuse and violence.

CHALLENGING BEHAVIORS

Defiance

When you are defiant, you tend to challenge authority figures such as parents, resist rules, and assert your independence. This can lead to conflicts and hinder your personal growth. This behavior can manifest as defiance or disobedience as you seek to establish your autonomy. When suffering from bipolar disorder, defiance can further be complicated by fluctuating mood swings and impulsivity.

Risk-taking behavior

As a teenager, risk-taking behavior can often be seen as a crucial way to challenge yourself and learn about your limits. You may engage in risky behaviors, such as experimenting with drugs and alcohol, and engaging in unsafe sexual practices, or participating in daredevil activities. This behavior is often driven by curiosity, peer pressure, and a desire for thrill and excitement.

When suffering from bipolar disorder, during a manic episode, you may engage in risky behaviors such as substance abuse. During depressive episodes, engaging in risky behaviors such as physical fights or lashing out might serve as a coping mechanism. These behaviors could worsen the already existing problems, such as emotional distress and strained relationships, especially with family.

Emotional intensity

The teenage era is crucial for hormonal changes and emotional development, which can contribute to heightened emotions and mood swings. You may experience mood swings, intense emotions, and rapid shifts in your emotional well-being. During manic episodes, you can experience intense emotions such as anger and euphoria, which can lead to reckless behavior. You may have challenges controlling your feelings. During depressive episodes, mood swings can show up as overwhelming sadness and hopelessness, which can also make it challenging to engage in regular daily activities.

Isolation

Some teenagers may withdraw from social activities or isolate themselves from friends and family.

While spending time alone can be healthy and helpful in self-reflection, excessive time alone can negatively impact your mental health and social well-being. Isolation intensifies challenges already faced by teens with bipolar disorders and underlying emotional struggles, such as depression, impaired social functioning, and challenges in academics. This can also create a cycle of loneliness and negative self-image.

Peer influence

This is where you do things you wouldn't normally do because you want to feel validated and accepted by others. You may adopt certain behaviors or attitudes to align with your peer group, even if those behaviors are considered risky or inappropriate, like smoking or doing drugs. During manic episodes, you may engage in risky behavior, make hasty decisions, or overlook consequences because you are susceptible to peer influence. During depressive episodes, you may withdraw from social interactions and peers, which can make it difficult to seek necessary support or engage in social activities because you might feel worthless and have low self-esteem.

Technology addiction

Teenagers often devote much time to their devices for texting, social media, or calls. Technological addiction can be used as a form of escapism, especially during emotional distress, and used to bring temporary relief from intrusive thoughts. With this prevalence, you may struggle with excessive screen time, which in turn can impact your sleep patterns, academic performance, and overall well-being.

Identity crisis

Teenagehood is a crucial phase for identity development; you get to explore and define yourself, your values, beliefs, and aspirations. During manic episodes, you might experience heightened self-confidence and grandiosity, leading you to adopt new identities. During depressive episodes, you might struggle with confusion about your identity and have low self-worth.

You are in the process of forming your identity. This exploration may involve trying different personas, experimenting with various interests, and questioning established values and beliefs. The stigma surrounding mental well-being can easily complicate the process of identity formation.

Unhealthy eating patterns

Some teenagers may develop unhealthy eating habits, such as skipping meals, engaging in restrictive diets, or overeating, as they navigate through mood swings and emotional irregularities. This can be attributed to factors such as peer pressure, social media influence, and convenience. This can also contribute to poor dietary choices that affect your overall well-being and impact body image concerns or stress.

Impulsive decision-making

Decision-making can be a challenge to teenagers. During adolescence, your brain is still developing, sometimes contributing to indecisiveness. When you have bipolar disorder, impulsive decision-making manifests itself in different ways, such as reckless spending, making drastic and sudden changes in goals, or even relationships.

For example, in manic episodes, you might decide to engage in risky activities like substance abuse without considering the potential consequences, while in depressive episodes, you may withdraw from people and things you once loved, choosing not to engage at all.

It's important to note that challenging behaviors in teenagers are a normal part of development, but persistent or severe issues may require professional intervention. Open communication, understanding, and support from parents, guardians, and educators can contribute to positive outcomes and help you navigate these challenges successfully. If behavioral concerns persist or escalate, seeking guidance from mental health professionals may be beneficial.

SIGNS AND SYMPTOMS OF CHALLENGING PERSONAL BEHAVIORS

Challenging behaviors can vary widely among teenagers, and not all challenging behaviors are indicators of or are attributed to bipolar disorder. As a teenager with bipolar disorder, you may exhibit difficult behaviors that are indicative of the mood fluctuations and emotional dysregulation associated with the condition.[1] It's crucial to understand that not all teenagers will display the same signs and symptoms, which one family finds acceptable and another challenging. However, here are common signs and symptoms.

Defiance

Defiance is a prevalent indication of challenging personal behavior observed in teenagers. It manifests when one refuses to adhere to rules or instructions, often coupled with an assertive or aggressive demeanor. The following outlines the manifestations of defiance in this context. How it appears:

Talking back
Defiance becomes evident through consistent arguments, relentless questioning of rules, or the expression of disrespectful remarks directed at parents, teachers, or other authority figures.

Refusal to cooperate
You may overtly reject tasks such as chores, homework completion, or adherence to established routines.

Passive-aggressive conduct
Compliance with requests may take a superficial form, marked by subpar effort, excessive procrastination, or a display of sullenness.

Nonverbal defiance

Forms of defiance extend to nonverbal expressions, including eye rolls, door slamming, or outright disregard for given instructions.

Changes in sleep patterns

Adolescents commonly grapple with sleep challenges, yet notable alterations in sleep patterns can indicate the presence of underlying challenging personal behaviors. Adolescents typically undergo a biological shift in their sleep cycle, leading to a natural inclination for later bedtime and waking hours. This shift is influenced by changes in melatonin production, a hormone crucial for regulating sleep-wake cycles.[2] Deviations from this norm can signal potentially challenging behaviors, indicating the importance of recognizing and addressing such signs. Indicators:

Difficulty initiating sleep

While grappling with challenging behaviors, you may find it difficult to sleep, which is often attributable to stress, anxiety, or depression, and in return can lead to prolonged periods of worry or overthinking.[3]

Excessive sleepiness

Conversely, some teenagers may exhibit heightened sleepiness, potentially signaling underlying concerns such as depression or substance misuse.

Irregular sleep routines

Frequent alterations in sleep schedules, like staying awake late one night and oversleeping the next, could indicate emotional regulation or difficulty coping with stress.

Impact on behavior

Ineffectual sleep can exacerbate pre-existing challenging behaviors. Sleep-deprived teenagers may showcase heightened irritability, impulsivity, or concentration difficulties that lead to escalating interpersonal conflicts.

Changes in activity levels

This can be indicative of underlying challenging personal behaviors, particularly concerning mental health or emotional issues. These shifts may manifest as hyperactivity, social withdrawal, alterations in participation, disrupted sleep patterns, impulsive behaviors, decreased academic performance, changes in exercise routines, isolation from hobbies, and inconsistent energy levels. These variations can signal potential mental health challenges such as anxiety, depression, ADHD, or mood disorders.[4]

Isolation

Isolating yourself could indicate an underlying challenging personal behavior, especially when you avoid spending time with your friends and family, withdraw from social interactions, or prefer to be alone. You could feel overwhelmed by emotions that may make you want to be alone to cope with those challenges.

Academic decline

As a teenager, you may start having difficulty concentrating, missing school days, arriving late, and exhibiting other behavioral issues, all of which are indicators of challenging personal behaviors. This, in turn, results in missed assignments, failure to catch up on coursework, and, ultimately, academic decline.

Substance abuse

This involves misuse or excessive consumption of drugs or alcohol. This sometimes comes as a means of coping with stress, numbing painful experiences, or escaping reality. This may also be accompanied by secretive behaviors and, at times, physical signs of intoxication.

Self-harm

Self-harming behaviors such as hitting yourself and the urge to cut yourself can be a way of coping with overwhelming psychological distress, especially during depressive episodes. It may also result from the need to release emotional pain, emptiness, or numbness.

It's important to recognize these signs early on and seek professional help. If you suspect you may have bipolar disorder, it's crucial to talk with a mental health provider to get a comprehensive evaluation and appropriate treatment. Early intervention and a combination of medication, therapy, and support can significantly improve outcomes for teenagers with bipolar disorder. Family support and education are also essential components of managing the condition effectively.

CAUSES OF CHALLENGING PERSONAL BEHAVIORS IN TEENAGERS

Challenging behaviors in teenagers, especially those with bipolar disorder, can stem from a blend of biological, psychological, and environmental elements. Exploring the causes reveals intricate connections.

Biological influences

Neurotransmitter imbalances

Bipolar disorder correlates with disruptions in neurotransmitters like serotonin, dopamine, and norepinephrine that affect mood regulation and contribute to challenging behaviors. [5]

Brain structure and function

Variations in brain structure and function, notably in areas such as the amygdala and prefrontal cortex, can impact emotional regulation and impulse control, giving rise to challenging behaviors.[1]

Genetic factors

Family history

A strong genetic link exists in bipolar disorder. Teenagers with a family history face an elevated risk, and genetic predisposition can shape the manifestation of challenging behaviors.[4]

Hormonal changes

Puberty impact

Hormonal shifts during puberty can intensify mood swings and emotional volatility, particularly affecting teenagers with bipolar disorder and amplifying challenging behaviors.[4]

Psychosocial elements

Family dynamics

The family environment is pivotal, with high stress, conflict, or dysfunction that contribute to challenging behaviors in teenagers with bipolar disorder.

Peer influences

Adolescence emphasizes peer relationships and negative influences or difficulties forming healthy friendships that can contribute to challenging behaviors.

Environmental stressors

Academic pressures
Stressors linked to academic expectations may trigger mood episodes and worsen challenging behaviors in teenagers with bipolar disorder.

Social stress
Challenges in social acceptance, bullying, or feelings of isolation may contribute to emotional dysregulation and problematic behaviors.[4]

Dual diagnosis

Substance abuse
Teenagers with bipolar disorder might resort to substance abuse as a way to self-medicate, thus amplifying challenging behaviors.

Coping mechanisms

Maladaptive coping strategies

To handle intense emotions, teenagers with bipolar disorder may develop maladaptive coping strategies, like impulsive actions or withdrawal, which can lead to challenging behaviors.

Individual personality traits

Temperament
Unique personality traits, such as impulsivity or high sensitivity to stress, can influence how challenging behaviors manifest in teenagers with bipolar disorder.

ADDRESSING CHALLENGING BEHAVIORS IN TEENS

Teenagehood is a time for growth, discovery, and change; however, being a teenager comes with unexpected challenges, not only physically but also mentally. Teenage behavior problems can be effectively addressed using personalized tactics, support networks, and therapeutic philosophies. Understanding that every adolescent is different and that what suits one may not suit another is critical. Here are some of the ways to help with treating these behaviors.

Psychotherapy

A key component of treatment for teens with bipolar disorder is psychotherapy. Interpersonal and Social Rhythm Therapy (IPSRT), Dialectical Behavioral Therapy (DBT), and Cognitive-Behavioral Therapy (CBT) are examples of therapies that can assist in creating routines, teach useful coping mechanisms, and help handle stress. Family-Focused Therapy (FFT), also helps lower recurrence rates and the intensity of symptoms for adults and adolescents.[6]

Try to defuse heated arguments

Being furious during a conversation usually results in a heated dispute that generates no results or undesired results. In most if not all situations, arguing rarely produces great results. Stay away from bugging others; they will eventually tune you out and stop listening, making you angrier. If the dispute is between you and a sibling, listen to their concerns, consider what's at stake, and find a settlement or a way to end the fight before it gets out of hand.

Try to diffuse the conflict rather than stir it up, by giving others space to talk freely and helping them reach a solution or conclusion. Try not to lose your cool when someone argues back or reacts angrily. Use humor to lighten the mood of a disagreement and reduce tension, but refrain from using derogatory or caustic language. When a disagreement gets too heated, leave the room and return to resume the conversation when you are both at ease.

Get support from a counselor if you frequently have heated disagreements and struggle to control your irritation or anger. A counselor can provide an impartial, unbiased opinion and suggest new strategies for managing anger.

Medication

Mood stabilizers and antipsychotic medications, which are frequently prescribed for adult bipolar disorder, have also been shown to be successful in treating teenage bipolar disorder.[7] However, because of possible adverse effects, both you and your parents might be worried about you taking medication. Talking openly and honestly with medical professionals about the advantages and disadvantages of medicine is crucial.

Boundaries

As you become older, you learn to be independent by growing apart from your parents, and it's critical that you get the flexibility and room to accomplish this. However, establishing boundaries is also crucial. Sometimes, you will attempt to push the limits to see how much you can get away with. At some point, you should include your parents in this process and establish clear guidelines. Establishing rules helps you understand what is expected of you and what happens if you choose to disobey them.

The best limits or regulations are reasonable, equitable, and easy to follow. You can support yourself by administering consequences consistently and whenever a rule is violated. Reacting to backtalk, disobedience, or bullying is not appropriate. Remember that disrespectful behavior has repercussions, and one of the best ways to act is by responding accordingly rather than overreacting or making the issue worse.

Aggression and violent behavior

As a teenager, you occasionally battle with feelings of resentment or rage that can lead you to act violently or aggressively toward those around you. You should understand that it is improper to use aggressiveness and violence towards anyone. Inform those around you that you are leaving and will come back when they have calmed down if they are acting aggressively against you. Among the techniques for handling your violent behavior are:

- Step away from the person escalating the situation and give them time to collect themselves before continuing the conversation. Always engage with them in a non-violent and courteous manner.
- You should understand that your aggressive behavior is unacceptable. You should establish suitable, non-violent consequences and follow through on them.

Lifestyle

Promoting healthy lifestyle choices has a big effect on your well-being. The three most important things in managing bipolar disorder are getting enough sleep, having a balanced diet, and regularly exercising.[6] Furthermore, fostering a caring and understanding environment at home might help you achieve general stability and healing.

See a doctor

Seek advice from mental health specialists who have treated teenagers with bipolar disorder. They can offer professional advice and assistance that are catered to your requirements. However, one question arises. When is the right time to see a doctor?[8]

Sometimes, severe and persistent challenging behavior can indicate a medical issue or a more serious social or emotional problem. A general physician can investigate this and refer you to a specialist if needed. You should speak with your physician if you are concerned that your behavior is linked to a mental health problem.

Behavioral challenges can have an ongoing, negative impact on social and family life. If you are having difficulties managing or coping with your challenging behavior, you can talk to a physician who may refer you to a specialist in pediatric behaviors.[8]

Build a positive relationship

You will be able to better handle challenging circumstances if you have the tools to develop resilience and coping mechanisms. Building resilience requires spending time with supportive friends, family, and peers and cultivating good relationships based on trust, respect, and mutual support. You can exhibit positive behaviors by:

- Promoting a balanced diet, regular exercise, and getting enough sleep.
- Talking freely about your issues, solving problems together with your peers, and first asking if they'd like your advice or opinion before giving it to them, as well as demonstrating interest in their life and acknowledging their accomplishments.
- Managing worry and stress by engaging in open communication about feelings or issues. Also, try spending time as a family and one-on-one with your parents and siblings.

If you're a teen and struggle to have a good connection or are frequently at odds, there may be another adult you can trust to support you and provide a good example—an aunt, family friend, or sports coach.

Patience and understanding

Managing bipolar disorder can be difficult. Always know that when things get tough, you can turn to your parents or a trusted adult or guardian who will be happy to help and support you.

Education

Spend some time learning about the signs and symptoms of bipolar disorder as well as available treatments. Having knowledge enables you to make wise choices about your treatment and therapy options.

Communication

Promote an open conversation inside the family. Talking about emotions and difficulties can promote empathy and a caring atmosphere. Being receptive to the ideas and feelings of others without passing judgment, helps provide a secure environment for teenagers to express themselves. This can in return improve relationships and offer emotional support.

Discuss and confront other occurring issues

Studies have indicated that bipolar disorder frequently coexists with other psychological diseases, such as addiction. Substance misuse problems increase the likelihood of bipolar illness in adolescents and can worsen the symptoms of both disorders.[4] It is crucial for you to recognize this relationship and act upon it right away. Try to find treatment for your condition and other problems if you notice that they are there. Effective and long-lasting recovery requires treating co-occurring disorders.

Having empathy, tolerance, and a commitment to your well-being is essential when dealing with bipolar disorder. You also need support from your parents, a trusted adult, or a guardian. These people can support you by gaining knowledge about bipolar disorder, recognizing its symptoms, and seeking appropriate treatment. Creating a supportive environment that fosters open and clear communication as well as understanding, can significantly impact your journey toward recovery and an improved quality of life.

Always remember that you are not navigating this path alone. Reach out to family, support groups, mental health professionals, and other teenagers who are undergoing similar struggles. By collaborating together, these support groups can assist you in overcoming the challenges posed by bipolar disorder and embracing a more promising future.

Self-awareness

Take time to reflect on your thoughts, emotions, feelings, and behaviors. Identify patterns, behaviors, or triggers that contribute to your challenging behaviors. When you understand yourself better, you can easily address the root causes of these behaviors.

Prioritize self-care

Make self-care a top priority in your everyday routine. Take care of your health—physical, emotional, and mental well-being, by sleeping and resting enough, eating healthy, nutritious foods, exercising regularly, as well as engaging in activities that promote relaxation and stress relief.

Challenge negative thought patterns and emotions

Pay attention to your inner voice and challenge negative emotions, thoughts, and beliefs that are contributing to your challenging behaviors. Practice daily affirmations and reframe negative thoughts into more positive and realistic ones.

Develop coping skills

Learn and practice healthy coping strategies to manage your emotions, stress, and difficult situations. Experiment with different strategies such as deep breathing, mindfulness, meditation, or progressive muscle relaxation to find what works best for you. What might work for someone might not necessarily work for you.

CHAPTER 5
CHOOSE CHANGE FOR YOUR THOUGHTS

B eing a teenager is tough enough by itself, but when you add bipolar disorder to the mix, it can feel overwhelming. The good news is you're not alone! Millions of other teens around the world experience bipolar disorder, but it doesn't have to define who you are. Even with bipolar disorder, you primarily think the same way as any other person; you're only different because of the moods that influence your thoughts and behaviors.

Have you ever stopped and considered the impact your thoughts have on your life? Understanding and actively choosing to change your thoughts can be a game-changer while dealing with bipolar disorder. Bipolar disorder messes with the way your brain processes information and regulates emotions. It can distort your thinking, making negative thoughts feel like a catchy pop song stuck on repeat. You might find yourself dwelling on past failures, convinced they define you. You worry about the future endlessly, or spiral into a relentless symphony of anxiety.

The way you think shapes everything in your life, including your bipolar disorder. Negative thoughts can fuel emotional storms; while positive ones can help you navigate those storms and even find sunshine in between. This chapter will be your guide to understanding how your thoughts impact your mood and how you can captivate the power of positive thinking to manage your bipolar disorder and build a life you love. Your thoughts are not just fleeting notions. They are building blocks of your emotions, behaviors, and ultimately the outcomes you experience in life.

This chapter is your guide to hitting stop on negative thoughts. There is remarkable healing and growth that happens when you consciously choose to shift your thought pattern. Whether you are dealing with mood swings, navigating challenging situations, or simply seeking greater fulfillment, the power to change your life lies within your mind. We'll explore how to identify those distorted thoughts, challenge their power, and choose a more empowering playlist for your mind.

Because, guess what? You don't have to stay stuck on shuffle. You have the power to curate your soundtrack, one that reflects your strength, resilience, and the amazing person you are—bipolar disorder or not.

Understanding the significance of changing thoughts can create a mindset that empowers one to overcome obstacles, embrace resilience, and cultivate the life desired.

THE IMPACT OF THOUGHTS ON TEENAGERS WITH BIPOLAR DISORDER

Your thoughts hold immense power over your emotions and behaviors, especially when dealing with bipolar disorder. Positive thoughts can uplift your mood and motivate you to take positive actions, while negative thoughts can spiral into feelings of despair and hopelessness. As a teenager with bipolar disorder, you may find yourself caught in a cycle of manic highs and depressive lows, often fueled by your thought patterns.

It's important to acknowledge that each person's thoughts are unique and deeply personal. What may seem like a minor issue to you, could trigger intense emotions and reactions in another. Your thoughts are valid and deserve attention, but they also have the potential to influence your mental well-being.

Imagine your brain as the mission control for your entire body. It sends electrical signals that tell your heart to beat, your lungs to breathe, and your muscles to move. But your brain also controls your emotions. Consider a sad memory—doesn't your chest tighten up? Or how about a funny joke—does it make you smile? These are all perfect examples of how your thoughts directly impact your feelings.

Now, let's add bipolar disorder to the equation. This condition causes extreme mood swings, but what triggers those swings? Often, it's our thoughts. During a manic episode, you might have racing thoughts that make you feel invincible and full of energy. But those same thoughts can also lead to risky behavior and eventually result in a depressive episode. Depressive episodes, on the other hand, can be fueled by negative self-talk like, "*I'm worthless*" or "*I'll never get better.*" These thoughts can make you feel hopeless and withdrawn, making it even harder to manage your bipolar disorder.

The good news is that just as your thoughts can trigger negative emotions, they can also trigger positive ones. Learning to recognize your thought patterns and actively choosing to change negative ones is a powerful tool in managing your bipolar disorder.

HOW THOUGHTS ALTER YOUR LIFE

Bipolar disorder in teenagers is a complex dance between brain chemistry, emotions, and thoughts. While biology plays a role, ultimately, it is our thoughts that act as a powerful filter, influencing how we perceive the world and navigate our emotional rollercoaster when living with bipolar disorder.

You have to know that mood is a state of mind and not a response to emotions. Mood affects your thinking patterns of decision-making that are primarily based on rational thought processes. During a manic episode, you tend to think differently from someone who is simply happy, while when you are in depressive episode, you tend to think differently from someone who is simply sad. The following is a closer look at how thinking shapes life for teens with bipolar disorder.

THE BIPOLAR ROLLER COASTER

Ups and downs caused by thoughts

Bipolar disorder causes extreme mood swings, but what brings about these shifts? Often, it's our thoughts. During a manic episode, as a teenager, you might have racing thoughts that make you feel invulnerable and take on risky behaviors. These same thoughts, however, can eventually lead to a depressive episode.

On the other hand, depressive episodes can be caused by constant negativity. At times, you might bombard yourself with thoughts like, "*I'm a failure*" or "*I'll never get through this*," leading to feelings of hopelessness and withdrawal.

Power of perception

Thoughts don't just trigger emotional episodes; they also shape how you perceive the world around you. For example, during a manic episode, you may view a simple challenge as an easy feat due to blown-up self-esteem. This distorted perception can lead to poor decision-making and negative consequences. While during a depressive episode, you may look at small problems as insurmountable challenges.

Cycle of negativity

Negative thought patterns can cultivate a vicious cycle. When experiencing a depressive episode, you might have negative thoughts about yourself, the world, and the future. These thoughts can result in a feeling of lack of motivation and hopelessness, which can worsen the negative thoughts, creating a downward spiral.

COMMON THOUGHT PATTERNS DURING BIPOLAR EPISODES IN TEENS

Bipolar disorder can be a tough journey for you as a teenager, with extreme mood swings impacting how you think about yourself and your surroundings. The rapid mood swings can trigger negative thought patterns that feel impossible to escape. Let's explore the common thought patterns teens experience during manic and depressive episodes.

Manic episodes

Racing thoughts

Imagine your mind is a busy highway during rush hour. Thoughts zoom by at breakneck speed, making it hard to focus on anything. Racing thoughts may lead to the generation of ideas so that you are frantically moving from one thought to the next. You might jump from one idea to the next, start projects you never finish, and have difficulty concentrating in school or with friends.

Inflated self-esteem

During a manic episode, self-doubt goes out the window. You might develop a sense of grandiosity, believing you have special abilities or talents that set you apart from everyone else. This inflated sense of self-importance can lead to bragging, bossiness, and difficulty taking criticism.

Decreased need for sleep

Sleep? Who needs it? The surge of energy during a manic episode can make you feel like you can function on minimal sleep or even no sleep at all, despite the body's need for rest. However, this lack of sleep can worsen symptoms and contribute to a depressive episode.

Pressured speech

Have you ever felt like you have a lot to say, but you can't get words out fast enough? Pressured speech happens when you talk fast and intensely to a point where others cannot understand you.

Loose association

This happens when your thoughts or speech barely relate to what has been said or the topic, making your conversation seem scattered.

Poor impulse control

The combination of racing thoughts, high energy, and inflated self-esteem can lead to impulsive decisions without considering the consequences. You might engage in risky behavior, spend money you don't have, or make reckless choices.

Unrealistic optimism

Everything seems possible during a manic episode. This, in turn, leads to unrealistic plans, taking on too many commitments, or believing you can achieve anything you set your mind to, regardless of the challenges involved. This unrealistic optimism can lead to disappointment and frustration when things inevitably don't go according to their grand plan.

Depressive episodes

Negative self-talk

Your inner critic constantly bombards you with negative thoughts, such as, "*I'm worthless,*" "*I'm a failure,*" or "*Nobody likes me.*" This negative self-talk fuels feelings of worthlessness and hopelessness. You might constantly dwell on past mistakes or feel like a burden to others.

Hopelessness and helplessness

The future seems bleak and devoid of any possibility of improvement. You might feel like things will never get better, no matter what you do. This hopelessness can lead to a lack of motivation and a sense of giving up.

Worthlessness and shame

Guilt and shame can become overwhelming burdens. You might believe you are a burden to others and that everything bad that happens is your fault. These feelings further isolate you and make it difficult to seek help.

Thought blocking

This is the feeling of being unable to think clearly or concentrate. For example, you could be talking to someone and cut off mid-thought. Then, you might need help finding words, making decisions, or completing tasks that require focus.

Loss of interest

Activities that were once a source of joy become uninteresting and unappealing. You might withdraw from friends, hobbies, and even school.

The downward spiral of negative thoughts

Triggering mood episodes

Negative thought patterns are a major trigger for mood episodes in bipolar. During a manic episode, thoughts like, *"I'm invincible"* or *"I can do anything"* can lead to risky behaviors and poor decision-making. On the other hand, depressive episodes can be created by relentless negativity. Thoughts like, *"I'm weak"* or *"I'll never get better"* can lead to feelings of hopelessness, withdrawal, and even suicidal thoughts.

Fueling anxiety and stress

Negative thoughts can also worsen anxiety and stress, which can further exacerbate bipolar disorder symptoms. For example, if you constantly worry about failing a test, you might experience heightened anxiety, thus impacting your ability to focus and study effectively.

Hindering recovery

Negative thinking can hinder your recovery from a mood episode. Believing you won't get better could make you lack motivation to participate in treatment or engage in healthy coping mechanisms.

HOW BIPOLAR TEENS THINK THEIR WAY THROUGH LIFE

Bipolar disorder in teens is a complex dance between thoughts, feelings, and actions. Your thinking patterns can have a dramatic impact on both the positive and negative aspects of your emotional state and behavior. Here's a breakdown of this crucial connection.

Building self-esteem

Teenagers with bipolar disorder often struggle with negative self-beliefs. Challenging these thoughts and replacing them with positive affirmations like, "*I can do this*" or "*I am worthy,*" can improve self-esteem and overall well-being. Positive self-talk can also empower you to take on challenges and pursue your goals.

Promoting healthy habits

Positive thoughts can motivate you to adopt healthy habits that can significantly impact your bipolar disorder. For example, thinking about the benefits of exercise, healthy eating, and enough sleep can encourage you to prioritize these behaviors, which will lead to improved mood stability.

Boosting mood

Positive thoughts can be a real mood elevator for you as a teenager with bipolar disorder. Encouraging self-talk like, *"I am strong"* or *"I can handle anything,"* can chip away at negativity and foster feelings of resilience.

VIEWING LIFE THROUGH CLARITY AND CHANGE WITH BIPOLAR DISORDER

Bipolar disorder can feel like riding a super intense emotional rollercoaster, with highs so high you touch the clouds and lows that sink you deep into the mud. It can be tough to see clearly through the fog of those extreme moods, but here's the good news: you're not stuck on this ride forever. By learning to view life through the lenses of clarity and change, you can take control and navigate those ups and downs like a pro.

Think of clarity as your superpower

Imagine you're putting on a pair of special glasses. These aren't just any glasses—they're clarity glasses! When you wear them, the world comes into sharper focus. You can see things for what they truly are, not how your mood might be warping your perception.

Calming the overactive mind

During a manic episode, your brain might be firing on all cylinders, throwing a million thoughts at you a minute. Clarity helps you slow down and sort through those thoughts. You can ask yourself questions like, *"Is that risky idea really a good one,"* or *"Is my racing mind tricking me?"* Clarity allows you to step back, analyze the situation, and make choices based on logic, not just your impulsive feelings.

Seeing the light at the end of the tunnel

Depressive episodes can make the future seem dark and hopeless. But with clarity glasses on, you can see that this feeling is temporary. You've gotten through tough times before, and you will again. Clarity allows you to recognize those negative thoughts and challenge them with a more realistic perspective.

EMBRACING CHANGES DURING THE JOURNEY

With the ability to look at things more clearly, you can see things more clearly. Now what? This is where change comes in as your co-pilot on this journey of managing your bipolar disorder.

Change doesn't have to be scary

It might seem easier to stick to your old habits, even if they're not helping you. But change brings about growth. Maybe you need to change your sleep schedule to get back on track or change your approach to studying that would better help you manage stress. Even minor changes can make a large difference in your mood and overall mental well-being.

Building healthy habits

Think of your brain like a muscle. The more you feed it with healthy habits, the stronger it becomes. As mentioned previously, healthy eating, regular exercise, and enough sleep are all crucial for managing bipolar disorder. Building these habits might take you some effort at first, but over time, they'll become second nature and help you feel your best.

Finding the right support system

You don't have to go through this alone.
Consulting a therapist can give you the tools you need
to manage your bipolar disorder and develop healthy
coping mechanisms. Your friends and family can also
be a great source of support. Let them in on what
you're going through, and don't be afraid to ask for
help when you need it.

IDENTIFYING THOUGHTS AND FEELINGS THAT CAN TRIGGER EPISODES

Bipolar disorder itself isn't caused by thoughts or self-
talk, but negative thought patterns can definitely
trigger mood episodes or worsen existing ones. The
following are some ways you can identify thoughts
that might be leading toward an episode.

Recognizing triggers

The first step is becoming aware of your inner
voice. Here are some tips.

Mood tracker
Keep a mood tracker where you record your
mood throughout the day. Next to each mood
entry, write down the thoughts you were

having just before. This can help you identify patterns between your thoughts and emotional state. To get you started, there are free mood tracker apps and printable versions available online.

The pause button

When you feel overwhelmed by negative emotions, hit the pause button! Take a deep breath and ask yourself, *"What thoughts are running through my head right now?"* Identifying the thought is the first step to challenging it.

Notice triggers

Be mindful of situations, events, or interactions that seem to change your mood. These triggers could be external factors like stress at school or conflicts with friends. It can also be internal factors like negative self-talk or unrealistic expectations.

Pay attention to physical symptoms

Notice how your thoughts are connected to physical sensations in your body. For exam-

ple, do you experience tension, a racing heart-
beat, or stomach discomfort when you have
certain thoughts? Physical symptoms can be
clues to underlying emotional processes.

Seek feedback

Talk to trusted friends, family members, or
mental health professionals about your experiences. They may be able to offer insights or
observations that you haven't considered.
Sometimes, an outside perspective can help
you recognize patterns that you may have
overlooked.

WATCH OUT FOR THESE THOUGHT PATTERNS

As a teenager, once you start recognizing your
thought patterns, be on the lookout for these common
thinking traps that can fuel bipolar episodes.

All-or-nothing thinking

Also known as black-and-white thinking, is when
you see things in extremes. You might feel terrible
because everything is not perfect, for example, "*This*

test is going to be a disaster" or *"I'll never get better."*
Challenge these thoughts by reminding yourself of
past successes or by focusing on smaller, achievable
goals.

Mind-reading

This happens when you assume you know what
other people are thinking. The thoughts are usually
negative about yourself, such as, *"Everyone thinks I'm
a failure."* Challenge these thoughts by reminding
yourself you can't control what other people think.

Catastrophizing

This usually occurs when you make a big deal out
of a small problem. For example, *"If I miss school,
I'm going to be dismissed from school completely."*
Challenge yourself by considering more realistic
outcomes and focusing on coping strategies.

Negative self-talk

This looks like having a constant reminder of
negative thoughts about yourself. Thoughts such as,

"*I'm worthless*," *"I'm a failure,"* and *"Nobody likes me,"* can be a major trigger for depressive episodes.

Inflated self-esteem

On the flip side, during manic episodes, grandiose thoughts of superiority or invincibility can be a red flag. Watch out for beliefs like, *"I can achieve anything without limitations"* or *"I don't need sleep."*

Overgeneralization

This happens when you relate everything with one experience, for example, *"I failed this test. Therefore, I'm going to fail the rest of them,"* or *"My medication doesn't seem to work, which means nothing will work. I just give up on feeling better."*

WAYS TO THINK POSITIVELY AND REDUCE ANY EPISODE-INDUCING THOUGHTS

Certainly, here are some strategies to help you think positively and reduce episode-inducing thoughts.

Mindfulness and meditation

Practice mindfulness and meditation to help yourself stay grounded and present in the moment. These practices can reduce stress, increase self-awareness, and promote a more positive outlook on life.

Cognitive Behavioral Therapy (CBT)

These techniques can help you challenge negative thought patterns and replace them with positive and realistic ones. Learning these strategies can be highly beneficial when working with a CBT-trained therapist.

Gratitude journaling

Keep a gratitude journal where you can write down things that you are grateful for each day. Focusing on the positives can shift your perspective and cultivate a more optimistic mindset.

Engaging in hobbies and activities

Be willing to participate in hobbies and activities that bring you joy and fulfillment. Enjoyable activities can distract you from negative thoughts and provide a sense of accomplishment and satisfaction.

Limiting negative influences

Identify and limit exposure to negative influences, such as negative news or negative social media content. Instead, surround yourself with positive people and uplifting content.

Setting realistic goals

Set realistic and achievable goals. Successes, no matter how small, can boost self-esteem and confidence, and reduce the likelihood of episodes that induce negative thoughts.

Seeking social support

Communicate openly with trusted friends, family members, or support groups. A supportive network can provide validation, understanding, and perspective during difficult times.

Creating a wellness routine

Establish a wellness routine that includes regular exercise, healthy eating, sufficient sleep, and relaxation techniques. Taking care of your physical and mental health can improve your mood and reduce the risk of episodes that induce these negative thoughts.

Identifying triggers

Identify triggers for negative thoughts or mood episodes. Once you have identified them, you can develop strategies to avoid or cope with them more effectively.

Seeking professional help

Remind yourself that it's okay to ask for help from mental health professionals when needed. Therapists, psychiatrists, and other healthcare providers can offer personalized support and treatment options to manage bipolar disorder effectively.

Positive affirmations

Repeating positive statements about yourself can help you build self-esteem and counteract negative self-talk. Our brains tend to concentrate on the negative, but you can change that by consciously making an effort to say good things about yourself.

By incorporating these strategies into your daily

lives as a teenager with bipolar disorder, you can cultivate a more positive mindset and reduce the occurrence of episode-inducing thoughts. It's important to approach these strategies with patience and consistency, as positive changes may take time to develop and maintain.

CHAPTER 6

PRACTICAL TIPS FOR MANAGING AND HEALING FROM BIPOLAR DISORDER

T his chapter is dedicated to providing practical tips for you, as a teenager, navigating life with bipolar disorder. In the journey of managing the complexities of the condition, having actionable strategies to overcome challenges and improve well-being is invaluable. This chapter aims to give you practical tips that go beyond mere suggestions, providing insightful perspectives and actionable steps to empower you to take control of your life and thrive despite the challenges that you may face.

Living with bipolar disorder can indeed feel like a constant struggle against unpredictable mood swings, overwhelming emotions, and the societal stigma asso-ciated with mental disorders. This can lead to a sense of powerlessness. However, it's essential to recognize that while the disorder may pose significant challenges, it does not define who you are or determine your future. By implementing practical tips and strategies, you can gain a sense of empowerment, allowing you to navigate life with greater confidence and resilience.

Each of the five practical tips presented in this chapter have been carefully selected to address key aspects of effectively managing bipolar disorder. While some tips may seem familiar, the ultimate goal is to offer fresh insights and perspectives that resonate with you and provide actionable steps for real-life application. Through detailed discussions and practical examples, this chapter aims to equip you with the tools you need to overcome obstacles, improve your mental well-being, and live a fulfilling life despite the challenges posed by bipolar disorder.

As you go through each tip, you should approach it with an open mind and a willingness to explore new ways of thinking and approaching challenges. Remember that managing bipolar disorder is a journey, and it's okay to seek support and guidance along the way. By embracing these practical tips and taking proactive steps toward self-care and personal growth, you can reclaim control over your life and build a brighter future filled with hope, resilience, and fulfillment.

TIP #1: PRIORITIZE MENTAL HEALTH AND MANAGE STRESS

An episode can be triggered by positive or negative stress since the brain and body respond to it identically. Stress can easily disrupt the delicate balance between mania and depression, resulting in episodes of either. These alternate periods are characteristic symptoms of bipolar disease.

The body releases a rush of hormones like cortisol and adrenaline when it experiences stress, triggering the fight-or-flight reaction.[1] Chronic stress can have a disastrous effect on the body and mind, even if this reaction is essential for survival in dangerous conditions. Stress can have an especially significant effect on those with bipolar disorder, who already exhibit heightened sensitivity to emotional and environmental stressors.

People with bipolar disorder may have more frequent and severe mood changes during stressful times. Stressful events, including relationship issues, financial hardships, or school-related stress, can set off manic episodes, which are marked by impulsivity, erratic behavior, and increased energy. On the other hand, stress can also trigger depressive episodes, which are characterized by extreme sadness, sluggishness, and hopelessness.

Bipolar illness symptoms can also be worsened by the physiological impacts of stress, which include changes in appetite, immune system suppression, and disturbed sleep patterns. Mood instability is closely associated with sleeping problems in particular, as irregular sleep patterns can throw off the body's circadian rhythm and lead to manic or depressive episodes.[2]

Therefore, prioritizing mental health and effective stress management plans are important to help with the treatment of bipolar disorder. By learning to cope with stress healthily, patients can attain greater stability and reduce the frequency and likelihood of mood episodes.

Mindfulness meditation

Mindfulness is one of the most effective stress management techniques. It is about living fully in the present moment, free from worries about the past or the future. Mindfulness is a lifeline, a beacon of awareness, illuminating the route to emotional equilibrium for people navigating the ups and downs of bipolar disorder. Imagine having the ability to see your thoughts and emotions as if you were a curious onlooker observing clouds as they moved across the sky

Bipolar patients who practice mindfulness might gain a fresh perspective and unravel the tangle of racing thoughts and fluctuating feelings. Mindfulness enables people to respond to stressors with calm and perspective, as opposed to behaving impulsively. It acts as a buffer against an onslaught of pressures that could destroy stability, much like a secret superpower. So, shut your eyes, inhale deeply, and let mindfulness lead the way as you go towards resilience and inner serenity.

Regularly engaging in physical activities

This is another powerful form of stress management. Whether you roll out your yoga mat or put on your trainers for a stroll, you're doing more than just exercising your body—you're releasing a stream of feel-good chemicals called endorphins. Consider them to be nature's mood boosters, sending waves of bliss signals into your brain and driving stress away.[3] But you don't have to limit yourself to anything. Do something you love

There are workouts out there for you. Whether it's

the pounding of your feet on concrete during a jog, or the contagious enthusiasm of a dancing class, the ultimate goal is about rediscovering your mind as a haven of fortitude and resilience, with joy in movement, instead of hurting yourself with exhausting exercises. Go out there and do something that makes your heart race and your emotions soar. With every stride, stretch, or shake, you're taking back control of your life and not simply controlling the symptoms of bipolar disorder.

Having a strong support network

Friends, family, and mental health professionals can provide invaluable emotional support during times of stress. Having someone to talk to, share experiences with, and seek guidance from, can significantly lessen the burden of managing bipolar disorder alone. In addition to mindfulness and exercise, maintaining a healthy lifestyle is crucial for stress management and overall well-being. This includes prioritizing adequate sleep and nutrition, as well as, limiting exposure to substances like alcohol and caffeine, which can exacerbate mood instability.

Even amid difficulties, people with bipolar disorder can empower themselves to lead happy, purposeful lives by learning these effective stress management strategies and developing resilience.

TIP #2: SHIFT YOUR FOCUS AND REFRAME MANIC AND DEPRESSIVE EPISODES

One powerful approach to managing bipolar disorder is through shifting your focus and reframing negative thoughts. By cultivating a positive outlook and adopting realistic and healthy thinking patterns, you can develop a renewed mindset that empowers you to navigate manic and depressive episodes more effectively.

It's very important to become familiar with your moods by monitoring and documenting them over time, typically in a journal or by using a phone app to record them. This allows you to identify patterns and acknowledge your triggers. Triggers can vary from feeling overwhelmed or stressed, to significant life events or changes in your physical or mental health. By recognizing these triggers, you can take proactive steps to manage your mood and prevent episodes from soaring. Here's a step-by-step approach to becoming a master of your mind.

Understanding your moods

The first thing you need to understand is that you have unique emotional patterns. Grab a journal or a mood-tracking app and become a detective of your moods! Track your emotions throughout the day. Note down situations that trigger manic episodes or make you feel depressed. Become aware of whether there are changes in your sleep or eating habits that might be early warning signals.

For example, maybe you notice that you get irritable, and your sleep gets disrupted before a manic episode. Recognizing these triggers is like identifying those pesky weeds in your garden—once you know where they pop up, you can take action before they take over.

Challenge those negative thoughts

It's important to understand that your brain often tends to be biased when it comes to negativity, meaning it dwells so much on the bad stuff more than the good. When a negative thought pops into your head, don't just accept it as truth. Challenge it! Ask yourself:

Is this thought realistic?
Maybe you're overwhelmed with schoolwork

and feeling overburdened. Instead of thinking, *"I can't do this, I'm going to fail,"* challenge that thought. Ask yourself, *"Is this really true?"* Can you break down the workload into smaller tasks? Could you talk to your teacher and ask for some extra help?

Is there another way to look at this situation? Let's say you had a little disagreement with a friend. Instead of dwelling on the negativity, try reframing the problem. Could this be an opportunity to talk things through and strengthen your friendship? Perhaps a misunderstanding took place that needs to be cleared up.

Refocus on the positive

Our brains naturally gravitate towards the negative. To cultivate a more positive outlook, make a conscious effort to shift your focus toward the good stuff. Here are some ways to do that.

Gratitude journaling
Write down three things you're grateful for, daily. It can be anything, big or small—a deli-

cious meal, a funny meme you saw online, or a supportive friend in your life. Focusing on gratitude can boost your mood and overall well-being.

Positive affirmations

Repeating positive affirmations to yourself can help refocus negative thoughts. For example, you could try affirmations like, "*I am capable*" or "*I am worthy of love and happiness.*"

Keep in mind that you are not your thoughts. Bipolar disorder might bombard you with negativity, but you have the power in you to challenge those thoughts and choose a healthier perspective. Think of it as weeding your mental garden and allowing the beautiful flowers of positive thoughts to bloom.

Dialectical Behavior Therapy

Dialectical Behavior Therapy (DBT) is a form of therapy that can be incredibly useful to people with bipolar disorder.[4] It is your toolbox for handling emotions. Think of DBT as a toolbox filled with skills to manage your emotions effectively. It is beneficial to discuss the benefits of talk therapy available for bipolar disorder, which can teach you the following skills.

Mindfulness

This skill teaches you to pay attention in the moment and observe your thoughts and emotions without passing judgment. Look at it as you would taking a step back from your thoughts and observing them like clouds passing by in the sky.

Distress tolerance

Life can be unpredictable, and sometimes you'll experience intense emotions. DBT teaches you healthy coping mechanisms instead of resorting to risky behaviors.

Emotional regulation

This skill helps you identify your emotions and learn how to handle these emotions healthily. For example, if you're feeling over-whelmed, you might learn calming techniques like deep breathing or relaxation exercises.

Interpersonal effectiveness

DBT equips you with communication skills to build and maintain healthy relationships.

TIP #3: CHANGE YOUR LIFESTYLE AND STICK TO A ROUTINE

Living with bipolar disorder can be challenging, especially for you as a teenager who is still navigating your way through the complexities of adolescence. However, establishing a consistent lifestyle and adhering to a routine can significantly improve the management of symptoms and the overall quality of life. Let's first discuss the practical benefits of changing lifestyle habits and sticking to a routine for someone with bipolar disorder.

Stability and predictability

Bipolar disorder often involves fluctuations in mood, energy levels, and behavior. By maintaining a stable daily routine as a teenager with bipolar disorder, you can create a sense of predictability in your life. This stability can help you regulate mood swings and reduce the risk of manic or depressive episodes.

Sleep regulation

Irregular sleep patterns can significantly impact bipolar symptoms. Establishing a consistent sleep schedule with set bedtimes and wake-up times will promote better sleep quality and mood stability. Adequate sleep is crucial for managing symptoms and improving overall mental health.

Healthy habits

Encouraging healthy lifestyle habits, such as regular exercise and nutritious eating, can have a positive impact on your mood and energy levels. Physical activity releases endorphins, which can help you alleviate symptoms of depression and anxiety. Similarly, a balanced diet provides essential nutrients that support overall well-being.[3]

Time management

A structured routine helps you to manage your time more effectively, reducing feelings of being overwhelmed and stressed. By breaking tasks into manageable chunks and scheduling activities throughout the day, you can maintain a sense of control over your responsibilities.

Social support

Engaging in social activities and maintaining connections with friends and family members can provide you with valuable support as you fight bipolar disorder. Including social interactions in your daily routine can foster a sense of belonging and reduce feelings of isolation.

Self-care practices

Incorporating self-care activities into your routine is essential for managing stress and promoting emotional well-being. Prioritize activities that you find enjoyable and relaxing, such as reading, listening to music, or spending time outdoors.

Flexibility

While sticking to a routine is important, it's also crucial to be flexible and adaptable. Life can be unpredictable, and unexpected events may disrupt the usual schedule. Change how you approach things whenever necessary and adjust your routine accordingly.

Think of routine as your best friend

Imagine your life as a well-oiled machine. Routine is the oil that keeps everything running smoothly. It provides structure, stability, and predictability, all crucial for managing your bipolar disorder.

Building your personalized routine

Your routine doesn't have to be rigid or boring! Think of it as a flexible framework. Here are some tips for building a routine that works for you.

Start small

Don't try to overhaul your entire life overnight; it takes time. Focus on one or two things at first, like going to bed and waking up at the same time each day.

Include fun stuff

Remember to schedule activities you enjoy! Make time for hobbies, socializing, and relaxing—these are also essential for your well-being.

Be flexible

Life happens! There will be days when sticking to your routine is impossible. Don't beat yourself up—just get back on track as soon as you can.

Get support

Talk to your parents, therapist, or doctor about creating a routine that fits your needs.

Benefits of having a routine

Improved sleep

A consistent sleep schedule is essential for mood stability. By going to bed and waking up at the same time each day, even on weekends, you're training your body to expect sleep at specific times. This can help regulate your sleep cycle, which can significantly impact your mood.

Reduced stress

Knowing what to expect each day can reduce feelings of stress and anxiety. Routine provides a sense of control, which is especially important for teens with bipolar disorder

who might feel like their emotions control
them.

Better mood regulation

Sticking to a routine can help prevent mood
swings from becoming too extreme. Regular
sleep, meals, and activities can help regulate
your body's natural rhythms, which can
contribute to more stable moods.

Increased energy levels

A consistent sleep schedule and healthy eating
habits, both supported by routine, can boost
energy levels throughout the day.

TIP #4: SURROUND YOURSELF WITH POSITIVE INFLUENCE AND BUILD A SUPPORT NETWORK

Struggling with bipolar disorder can be a lonely journey, but here's the good news, you don't have to go
through it alone. Building a strong support network is
like creating a squad of personal superheroes, ready to
catch you when you fall and celebrate your victories.
Navigating life with bipolar disorder can be challenging, especially as a teenager who is still developing
coping mechanisms and self-awareness.

One practical tip that can greatly benefit teenagers with bipolar disorder, is surrounding themselves with positive influences and building a strong support network. Here, you get to explore the importance of positive influences and supportive relationships in managing bipolar disorder, providing detailed insights into how you can cultivate a network of support to help you cope with the challenges you may face.

Why positivity matters

Humans are social creatures, and the people we surround ourselves with significantly impact our mood and well-being. Imagine this, you're feeling down about a depressive episode. If you spend time with someone who constantly criticizes or brings negativity into your life, they will likely worsen your mood. On the other hand, surrounding yourself with positive, supportive people has the opposite effect. They uplift you, encourage you, and remind you of your strengths. This positive influence is crucial for managing the emotional ups and downs of bipolar disorder.

Who's on your team?

Your support network is like a personal A-team, with different members playing different roles.

The inner circle

Family and friends are your closest companions, the ones who know you best and love you unconditionally. Sharing your struggles with them can be incredibly cathartic. Their understanding and support can be a powerful buffer against the challenges of bipolar disorder.

The coach

A therapist is your trained professional cheerleader and guide. They can provide individual therapy to teach you coping mechanisms, communication skills, and strategies for managing your bipolar disorder. Think of them as your trainer for mental well-being.

The tribe

Connecting with others who understand and are going through what you're going through is a game-changer. Support groups provide a safe space to share experiences, learn from others, and feel less alone. Hearing stories of triumph from others with bipolar disorder can be incredibly motivating.

Building your dream support team

Creating a support network takes time and effort, but here's how to get started.

Open up & be vulnerable

This might be the hardest part, but also very important. Talk to the people you trust about your struggles with bipolar disorder. Be honest with them about your condition and the kind of support you need. You might be surprised by how willing loved ones are to help.

Seek professional help

Talk to your doctor and family about getting a referral to a therapist specializing in bipolar disorder. A therapist can be a valuable asset in your support network, providing guidance and support, tailored to your needs.

Explore support groups

There are online and in-person support groups specifically designed for teens like you living with bipolar disorder. Ask your doctor, therapist, or school counselor for recommendations. You can also search online using reputable mental health organization websites.

Beyond just talking

Building a support network is more than just having people to talk to. These are the qualities to look for in your support system.

Supportive

Your support system offers you encouragement without judgment and listens patiently during tough times.

Understanding

They are willing to learn about bipolar disorder and how it affects you. They don't expect you to *"get over it."*

Respectful

They respect your boundaries and privacy. They understand that there might be days when you don't feel like talking, and that's okay.

Here's a breakdown of why and how to build a strong support network

Emotional support

Having a support network of friends, family members, teachers, and mental health professionals can provide invaluable emotional support for teenagers with bipolar disorder. These individuals can offer understanding, empathy, and encouragement during difficult times, helping to alleviate feelings of loneliness and isolation.

Practical assistance

Supportive people within the network can also offer help with daily tasks, such as schoolwork, household chores, or transportation. This can help you manage the stress of depressive episodes and reduce feelings of overwhelm, allowing you to focus on effectively managing your symptoms.

Positive influence

Surrounding yourself with people who have positive influences can profoundly impact your mental health and well-being. Positive influences can include friends who offer encouragement and motivation, family members who provide stability and unconditional love, and mentors who offer guidance and inspiration.

Role models

Building a support network can also provide you with access to positive role models who have successfully navigated living with bipolar disorder or other mental health challenges. These individuals can offer valuable insights, advice, and hope for the future, serving as sources of inspiration and motivation.

Validation and understanding

Sometimes, others might misunderstand or invalidate you. A supportive network can validate your experiences and feelings, helping you feel heard, accepted, and understood.

Reduced stigma

Surrounding yourself with supportive people who are educated about bipolar disorder can help you reduce the stigma and discrimination associated with the condition. This can create a more inclusive and understanding environment in which you will feel comfortable seeking help and support.

Professional support

In addition to friends and family, you must have access to professional support from mental health professionals, such as therapists, psychiatrists, or support groups. These people can offer specialized guidance and treatment to help manage symptoms and improve overall well-being.

TIP #5: FACE YOUR FEARS AND STAND UP FOR YOURSELF

Bipolar disorder can feel like a spotlight constantly shifting, highlighting your strengths one moment, and then illuminating your vulnerabilities the next. Fear, in particular, can become a blinding force, preventing you from experiencing life to the fullest. But here's the good news: you have the power to step out of the shadows and into the light. This tip is all about facing your fears and standing up for yourself. It might sound daunting, but it's a crucial step in taking

control of your bipolar disorder and building a
fulfilling life.

What does "facing your fears" mean?

Facing your fears isn't about becoming a fearless
superhero. It's about acknowledging the things that
make you anxious or uncomfortable and taking steps
to overcome them, even when it feels scary. This
might involve tackling specific situations in your
daily life, such as the following.

Public speaking
Does the thought of giving a presentation in
class or ordering food at a restaurant make
your palms sweat? You're not alone. Public
speaking anxiety is a common fear, but with
practice and preparation, you can develop the
skills to manage it.

Talking about your bipolar disorder
Opening up to friends and family about your
diagnosis can feel like a vulnerability, but it's
an important step in building a strong support
network. The people who care about you will

want to understand what you're going through and how they can best support you.

Setting boundaries

Knowing how to say "no" and setting boundaries with friends, family, and even classmates is crucial for your mental well-being. Bipolar disorder can be draining, and it's important to prioritize your needs and well-being.

Why face your fears?

The benefits of facing your fears are numerous, especially for someone with bipolar disorder.

Increased confidence

As you overcome challenges and conquer your fears, your confidence will naturally grow. You'll start to believe in yourself and your ability to handle difficult situations, both with and without bipolar disorder.

Reduced anxiety

Fear often fuels anxiety, creating a vicious cycle. By facing your fears head-on, you'll be better equipped to deal with anxiety-provoking situations in the future.

Stronger relationships

Being open and honest about your bipolar disorder can strengthen your relationships with loved ones. When you share your struggles, they can offer support and understanding, creating a stronger bond.

Greater independence

The more comfortable you become in different situations, the more independent you'll feel. You'll be able to navigate life's challenges with confidence, knowing you have the right skills to cope with whatever comes your way.

Facing your fears isn't about becoming perfect. It's about taking small steps towards a life where fear doesn't control you. With each step you take, you'll gain more confidence and feel empowered to live life on your terms, shining your light brightly, despite the challenges of bipolar disorder.

How to face your fears

Identifying and addressing fears

Bipolar disorder can amplify feelings of anxiety and insecurity, making it crucial for you to confront your fears proactively. Whether it's social anxiety, fear of judgment, or apprehension about specific situations, acknowledging and targeting these fears is the first step toward overcoming them.

Gradual exposure

Facing fears doesn't mean diving headfirst into the most daunting situations. Instead, it involves gradually exposing oneself to feared situations or activities, starting with manageable steps. For example, if a teenager fears speaking in public, they can begin by practicing in front of a trusted friend or family member before gradually increasing exposure.

Seeking support

Building a support network of friends, family, or mental health professionals can provide invaluable assistance in facing fears. These individuals can offer encouragement, guidance, and reassurance, helping the teenager navigate challenging situations with greater confidence.

Communication and advocacy

Standing up for oneself involves effectively communicating needs, boundaries, and preferences to others. For teenagers with bipolar disorder, this may include advocating for accommodations in school or work settings, expressing triggers and warning signs to friends and family, as well as seeking support during difficult times.

Self-compassion and resilience

Teenagers with bipolar disorder need to practice self-compassion and resilience as they confront fears and advocate for themselves. They may encounter setbacks along the way, but viewing these experiences as opportunities for growth and learning can foster greater resilience and confidence.

Celebrating progress

Each step taken toward facing fears and asserting oneself is worthy of celebration. By acknowledging and celebrating progress, teenagers can reinforce their efforts and build momentum toward overcoming future challenges.

Empowerment and freedom

Overcoming fears and standing up for yourself can lead to a sense of empowerment and freedom. Teenagers with bipolar disorder who confront and conquer their fears, gain a greater understanding of control over their lives, and an increased ability to pursue their goals and aspirations.

CHAPTER 7
APPLICATION IN YOUR CURRENT SITUATION

As a teenager, you are completely responsible for your behavior. Start by accepting that you are in charge of your actions, thoughts, and behaviors. No one can take care of this but you. You have to start by taking responsibility. Once you internalize this truth, it becomes much easier to deal with bipolar disorder.

Indeed, bipolar disorder is going to be an intrinsic part of your identity once you are diagnosed, but it doesn't define who you are. Embracing this truth will empower you and ultimately lead to holistic growth.

Try saying this:*"I have bipolar disorder, but I am 'insert your name!'"* For example, I can say, *"I have bipolar disorder, but I am Natasha!"*

When you start thinking of your diagnosis like

this, it becomes nothing more than a piece of you and your story, instead of defining who you are. It makes your bipolar diagnosis easier to think about and digest. This small change in language and definition can have a powerful impact because it leads to a powerful shift in identity. Learning to accept bipolar disorder helps break the existing self-stigmatizing beliefs—just like you would if you had allergies, were an introvert, or were near-sighted. What's more, it leads to a healthier self-image, which in return, helps you find ways to grow, despite the diagnosis. It can also open pathways to a more fulfilling life.

In this section, we'll discuss the application side of things—how you can apply different tips and strategies to your current situation, so you can consider who you are in light of this complicated truth and embrace changes in your life by taking small steps every day.

APPLICATION #1: PRIORITIZE MENTAL HEALTH AND MANAGE STRESS

Your body, mind, and spirit are completely dependent on your mental health. Your mental health, therefore, affects your overall well-being—feelings, actions, and behaviors. When your mental health isn't great, your physical health and relationships suffer. Bipolar disorder can indeed impact how you feel toward the people around you and how you interact with and think about them. It's also true that everyone can struggle with their emotional and mental health. Unchecked, your mental health can disrupt your life and the lives of people around you. For this reason, you must prioritize your mental health. How can you do this?

Speak kindly to yourself

Speaking kindly to yourself has some powerful benefits. It can calm your heart rate and help you move away from the fight-or-flight mode. To do this effectively, you need practice, and the best place to start is awareness. Pay attention to your thought patterns and how you speak to yourself. Is your internal dialogue kind or unkind? Is it compassionate or judgmental? Is it empathetic or harsh? Reframe your unkind thoughts with more understanding and compassionate thoughts.

Put your internal dialogue through the "friend test." Would you say that to your best friend? If you wouldn't, then don't speak like that to yourself. Instead, think about how you would talk to and support a friend dealing with the same problem.

Love your body

What do you see when you look at yourself in the mirror? This isn't a question asked philosophically but in a more literal sense. Do you love yourself? Or you don't. When you look at yourself in the mirror, do you notice your flaws, or do you appreciate how you look? Do you wish you had a smaller nose, a broader chest, thinner legs, or a taller frame?

Research indicates that the degree to which people are concerned about their body varies widely, from some simply not liking a single feature of their body, to the more complex mental health disorder known as body dysmorphia, in which people obsess about their physical appearance in a toxic way.[1] The truth is, that body image issues aren't just superficial; they can affect many areas of a person's life. This also means that loving your body will have a healthy impact on both your mental and physical well-being.

Start by practicing body gratitude. Work on being grateful instead of being critical. It's true that expressing gratitude and appreciation for your body can actually help you love yourself more and boost your body image.[1]

You can also get into a routine, such as being grateful every morning or evening as you are dressing up or brushing your teeth. The goal here is to pair gratitude with a habit that has already stuck from daily practice. In doing this, the already established habitual behavior will serve as a reminder for you to always be grateful for and love your body.

Do something that will make you feel confident

"I know I'll be more confident when… I get better grades or lose weight or get my first job!" Yes, we've all been there. Many of us tend to think that confidence should result from something outside ourselves. You may feel good when you do well in an exam, lift heavier weights at the gym, or get a new hairstyle or haircut. But this isn't true confidence because it can easily fade away when that feeling of success wears off.

True confidence is an outcome of your internal environment—your thoughts, actions, and behavior. It is in believing in yourself and your ability to excel.

One of the best ways to become more confident is to nurture the relationships we have with family, friends, and peers. It's easy to feel confident when you are surrounded by people who love and support you, particularly when you are dealing with a complex disorder such as bipolar disorder. Spend time with people who believe in you when you don't feel confident in yourself. Other things you can do to boost your confidence from the inside include:

- Work on being the best version of yourself —don't compare yourself with others. Instead, look at your strengths and achievements and all the things you love about yourself.
- Get rid of negative self-talk, as stated in the first point.
- Take a slow, deep breath whenever you feel anxious, worried, or overwhelmed.

Do not blame others for your well-being; it is your priority to focus on yourself first

You've probably heard the following quote:

"With great power comes great responsibility."
   - Marvel Comics

This quote has been repeated many times, but there's a better version of it that I love more:

"With great responsibility comes great power."
   - Unknown

The more responsibility you take for your life, the more power you have over your life. The first step toward solving a problem is accepting responsibility and your part in it. Many people hesitate to take responsibility for their lives because they believe that in taking responsibility, they are also admitting fault.

Indeed, fault and responsibility appear together in our culture, but they are very different. For example, if someone hits you with their car, they would be at fault and also legally responsible for compensating you for the damage caused. Yes, it was an accident, but they are still responsible. This is how fault works in our culture. If you do something wrong, you are on the hook and must make it right. This is how it should be.

Still, there are certain issues that we may not be at fault for, but we still have responsibility for them. For example, if you are diagnosed with bipolar disorder, it wouldn't be your fault that you wound up with a complex condition, but living with it would now be your responsibility. You have a choice about what to do next. Whatever you decide to do about it, whether that be choosing to accept the diagnosis, reject it, look for help, or ignore it, comes with its consequences. Sometimes, we find ourselves at fault for experiences that we didn't choose—this is life.

There is a big difference between blaming others for your situation and them actually being responsible for it. In truth, no one is responsible for your situation but yourself. Indeed, someone else may be to blame for your sadness, anger, or self-doubt, but no one is responsible for your anger or sadness. That's because you have a choice—choosing how you see things and react to them. The metric you use to measure your experiences is completely on you.

Why is it so easy for us to take responsibility for success and the nice things that happen to us? We often fight over who will take responsibility for the positive things and the happiness. Why isn't the same energy translated to mistakes and negative outcomes as well? Taking responsibility for your problem is far more superior and important. This is where true learning starts. That's where real-life improvement

occurs. For this reason, blaming others only
hurts you.

Learn to avoid, manage, and look after yourself when you feel stressed

The stress associated with bipolar disorder and its
accompanying symptoms may lead to behavioral,
physiological, and emotional consequences. You may
become withdrawn, aggressive, unmotivated, anxious,
depressed, and have difficulties with concentration
and problem-solving. How can you avoid, manage,
and look after yourself when this happens?

Well, you can start by avoiding anything that can
trigger or aggravate your stress, such as alcohol and
drugs. Instead, work towards eating a balanced diet,
getting enough sleep, and exercising regularly.

Try engaging in meditative and muscle relaxation
practices. You can pray, swim, walk in nature, listen
to calming music, or just sit in silence whenever you
feel overwhelmed.

Take a break to reorganize, rethink, reenergize,
and refocus on your actions and thoughts. This can
help you avoid and manage stress.

Seek help and support whenever you feel overwhelmed. Talk to a professional, your parents, or a

friend when you are struggling. This could help you lighten the mental load and find different approaches to dealing with the problems.

Find a routine that works for you and stick with it. Try your best to wake up and go to bed at the same time or at least around the same time daily. Drink enough water and eat at least three healthy meals, daily.

APPLICATION #2: SHIFT YOUR FOCUS AND REFRAME MANIC AND DEPRESSIVE EPISODES

You have more control over your thoughts than you believe.

We've all been there—suddenly, your thoughts take a negative, downward turn and stay there. This may happen frequently, especially when you are in a depressive episode. Still, these negative thoughts don't have to dictate your actions and thoughts. You can find ways to shift your mindset and think about the positive aspects of your life in a way that helps you reframe your negative thought patterns. When you learn to shift your focus and reframe your depressive episodes, you'll build resilience and a great sense of control. How can you do this?

**Identify the thoughts that are causing your
episodes (manic or depressive)**

Manic episodes are different; they result in high
energy levels—physically and mentally. The high
energy could lead to racing thoughts, impulsivity
leading to irrational decisions, euphoria (extreme
happiness), and high creativity. When do such
thoughts crop up in your mind? Take note of that as
well and write the thoughts down.

The depressive episodes associated with bipolar
disorder may lead to negative thought patterns such as
thoughts of self-harm, suicide, and delusions. These
negative thoughts can be overwhelming. Start by
identifying how and when those thoughts start.

When do negative thoughts pop into your mind?
Pay close attention to that. The thought could be
about your diagnosis, yourself, your future living with
bipolar disorder, or even your loved ones. To change
negative thoughts, you must first identify them. Once
you have identified that, grab a notebook and write
the thought down. You can also opt for a note-taking
app on your phone or computer. This is how you
recognize patterns and triggers.

In doing this, you'll reframe your thinking into

understanding that the thoughts associated with manic and depressive episodes aren't always true.

Challenge those thoughts that are causing your episodes

You have the negative thoughts and the accompanying episodes written down. Now, challenge those thoughts. Ask yourself whether or not those thoughts are true and accurate. *"Is this true?" "Is there evidence to support this thought?"* Often, you'll find that the negative thoughts result from emotions and feelings rather than real facts. Make this a habit—every time a negative thought pops up, write it down and challenge it. In doing this, you'll reframe your thinking into understanding that the thoughts associated with manic and depressive episodes aren't always true.

Identify helpful and realistic ways of thinking and dealing with this disorder

For every negative thought written down, find an opposite and more realistic counterpart to replace it with. This isn't to say that you should ignore everything you are thinking or all of your problems.

Instead, this is about learning to view the thoughts resulting from your episodes in a more balanced and realistic way.

For example, if you start thinking, *"My friends don't like me because I have bipolar disorder,"* consider alternative possibilities such as, *"My friends know about my bipolar disorder diagnosis, and they try to be as understanding as they can. I must also try to understand them and communicate clearly so they can support me better when I am dealing with different episodes."*

Build habits to replace thoughts with realistic and more positive ones

Identify positive habits that will help you overcome your negative thoughts.

One good habit you can try, is taking a break whenever a negative thought comes up. Stop, take a break, and count to five. During your break, try going back to points one and two—write the thought down and challenge it. The brief and seemingly insignificant break can be impactful. It can help you put a stop to your negative thought patterns, which would otherwise spiral out of control. Now, you have a chance to rethink and reframe your thoughts.

Gratitude. Start practicing gratitude. Gratitude is a powerful way to reframe your thoughts, even when you are in the midst of a manic episode or dealing with a depressive episode. Gratitude is an effective way to shift your thoughts from what's wrong in your life to what's actually great in your life. For example, what things are you happy to have in life? Write that down in your notebook. What people are you glad to have in your life? What things did you enjoy doing today? Start your day with gratitude—list all the things for which you are grateful. End your evenings the same way, too.

Writing. Journaling your thoughts, emotions, and ideas can be a great outlet. It can also help you keep track of your thoughts and emotions so you can identify triggers and episodes. Write the negative thoughts and the more realistic and positive ones you are replacing them with. Journaling like this will give you clarity and thought so you can track progress.

Celebrate and acknowledge progress, no matter how small. You successfully reframed a bad thought? Celebrate that. Have you successfully practiced gratitude? Acknowledge that! You've been journalling consistently for a while? Celebrate that too. Research has shown that celebrating the positive outcomes in our lives is impactful. It can motivate you to do more of the positive things, knowing that you'll be rewarded for it.[2] Do something you love—go to the movies, buy yourself flowers or chocolate, go out with friends, or go hang out somewhere you love either alone or with others.

Focus on building positive thought patterns intertwined with realistic and healthy thinking

Build positive thoughts and connect them with realistic, positive, and healthy thinking. This will take time, as any habit does.

Start by identifying areas that need change. If you want to build a more optimistic mindset, identify areas that you are negative about. Is it your school, body, family, or friends? Start by working on one area that needs a mindset shift and then replace the negative thought about that area with a positive or grateful thought. For example, when you think, "*I hate my school,*" start working on replacing that thought with, "*I'm glad I get to meet my friends and hang out with them in school,*" or "*I'm thankful to have the opportunity to receive an education.*"

Check yourself, as already mentioned in the second point. Evaluate your thoughts throughout the day. Challenge your negative thoughts and put a positive spin on them.

Open yourself up to humor. It's okay to laugh, smile, and be happy. Give yourself permission to do that, especially during the difficult days. Seek laughter in the things happening around you. Laugh at life and laugh at yourself as much as you can. In doing this, you will feel less stressed and cope better.

More importantly, surround yourself with like-minded people—positive people. The people around you must be supportive, dependable, and understanding. Make sure those people can give positive, helpful advice when things get tough. It's impossible to be positive around negative people. Instead, negative people will drain you and make you doubt yourself and your ability to cope and deal with your disorder positively.

Understand what causes triggers and mood changes

Lifestyle factors and changes play a significant role in the onset of mood and emotional changes. Intense physical, mental, and emotional factors can also lead to triggers and mood shifts. Common factors include:

- Feeling overwhelmed or busy.
- Stressful periods.
- Poor nutrition (which may lead to high or low blood sugar levels), as sugar is a well-known mood trigger.
- Significant life events (weddings, having a child, losing a loved one, etc.)
- Periods of change or uncertainty.
- Substance use and abuse.
- Hormonal imbalance.
- Lack of sleep.
- Physical or mental health issues.
- Changes/problems with treatment for bipolar disorder, even when taken as directed by a healthcare provider.

Once you've identified triggers, write them down and keep track of the accompanying mood changes. After a while, patterns may start to emerge, and you'll be able to know when an episode is imminent and what you can do to cope better.

If you have a great sense of what causes your mood swings or what triggers your episodes, you can find ways to manage and cope better with the emotional changes. Try experimenting with different approaches such as:

- Exercising regularly.
- Healthy diet changes—cutting out alcohol, too much sugar, and caffeine from your diet.
- Learning positive stress management techniques such as meditation, gratitude, or walking in nature.
- Adjusting your morning and night routine so you can get enough quality sleep.

Learn warning signs to help you better react before an episode

It's possible to impede the progress of an episode through early intervention. To do this, you must first learn to identify early warning signs of an approaching episode. One of the most challenging realities of living with bipolar disorder is that those who have it, lack proper knowledge, insight, and understanding. This means that their mood radar may stop working when they are dealing with major episodes. Consider talking with a close loved one who can give you objective insight when you aren't able to see things clearly. The earlier you get an intervention, the better chances you have of preventing an intense, full-blown episode. An episode (unless major), may

not be easy to identify. Always look out for significant changes in:

- Sleeping patterns.
- Eating patterns/appetite.
- Behavior.
- Social interactions.
- Weight.
- Mood anxiety, anger, or irritability.
- Speech.
- Concentration and decision-making.
- Memory.
- Self-esteem.

One of the most important things to monitor is
sleep. Needing less sleep is particularly an important
sign. It is also easier to see compared to other symptoms. Keep track of how much sleep you need versus
what you are getting. This could be a valuable asset in
identifying receding, existing, and impending
episodes.

Using Dialectical Behavioral Therapy (DBT)

DBT is a unique type of psychotherapy, also
known as a form of talk therapy, that is often used to

help people of all ages learn to manage moods.[3] It also borrows a lot from Cognitive Behavioral Therapy (CBT). DBT leans more towards a psychosocial treatment approach which prioritizes four therapeutic settings:

- Core mindfulness.
- Distress tolerance.
- Emotional regulation.
- Interpersonal effectiveness.

Through these approaches, you may learn to challenge unhelpful thought patterns and distortions so you can change your emotions and behaviors. You may also learn to regulate your emotions and develop reasonable and effective coping strategies that can help you solve your issues efficiently. Through DBT, you will also learn to:

- Become more mindful/aware of emotions and thoughts.
- Manage emotions instead of dwelling on painful emotions or trying to get rid of them.
- Cope with strong emotions in healthy ways.

- Set up routines that help keep moods stable.
- Be patient and kind to yourself.
- Care for yourself in positive ways.
- Get along with others better.

APPLICATION #3: CHANGE YOUR LIFESTYLE AND STICK TO A ROUTINE

Positive life changes can have a significant impact on your life. Making those changes can help you flourish, even when dealing with a complex disorder such as bipolar disorder. Still, this won't be easy, and it won't happen overnight. You'll have to put in the work consistently because some habits take a while to stick. If you find yourself struggling, try starting small. Try working on one new habit each week or month. This way, you'll not overwhelm yourself trying to get everything done at once. You can also just tweak things you already do in your daily routines.

There are also lifestyle indicators that may show that it's time to make lifestyle changes for the better. Some of them include:

- Low energy and motivation.

- Loss of joy in the things you used to love doing.
- Unhealthy friendships and relationships.
- Feeling unfulfilled or unhappy.
- Substance use and abuse.
- High levels of stress.
- Feeling low.
- Concerns about your physical health.

This list isn't exhaustive. You may experience other things to indicate that it's time to make a lifestyle change. If, at one point in your life, you ever feel like you are not living your best life physically, mentally, emotionally, spiritually, in your relationships, or at work (if you have a job), then it's time to make a life change.

Be mindful of what you put in your body (certain foods, drugs, alcohol, etc.)

Your eating habits have a direct and powerful impact on your physical and mental health. As we know, the two feed off of each other. If your mental health isn't good, you may not feel good physically, and when you aren't in great physical shape, you may not feel well mentally. The things you consume (not just food), have a direct impact on how much sleep you get and how much energy you have for the next day's challenges.

A balanced diet will improve your general quality of life. Do your research on healthy foods. Talk to your doctor and/or nutritionist about the best types of food to eat, given your diagnosis. There are many diets out there targeting different areas of our health, such as gut health, physical health, and inflammation, among other things. Besides, everyone is different; what may be considered healthy to one may be harmful to another, such as in the case of allergies.

Generally, the Centers for Disease Control and Prevention, argues that it is best to avoid foods that are high in fats, processed sugars, and sodium. One way to be mindful of what you consume is to lean more toward nutrient-dense meals that are rich in fiber, proteins, minerals, and vitamins. Don't forget to drink enough water as well.[1]

Still on that, what you consume isn't just limited to food. What are you listening to, watching, and reading? Are these things building you into being a better person? Always remember that if it's not adding to your life, then it's probably subtracting from it. There are lots of great videos you can watch and books to read. Always try to make the right choice.

Slowly incorporate exercise into your activities (this can look like walking, running, cycling, etc.)

Exercise is powerful and will greatly impact your physical, mental, and emotional health. There is enough evidence to show that exercise has a direct positive impact on quality of life.[4] Exercise can keep you driven and motivated, so you always have the energy to do things you love. Moreover, exercise leads to the release of the feel-good hormones known as endorphins, which generally improve mental health. The feel-good hormones can also boost your confidence and self-esteem, which can come in handy when you are dealing with depressive thoughts.[5]

If you've identified an activity you love, make it part of your routine—it could be yard work, swimming, weight lifting at the gym, daily walks, or jogging. Also, create an exercise log and/or journal to track your progress and improve accountability. If you find yourself struggling at first, try something light you can do at home. Stretching will help strengthen your muscles and feel stronger even as you work towards more complex exercises.

Incorporate self-care (skincare, hair care, etc.)

Sometimes, you may struggle with your mental health or experience burnout because you need a break. Maybe you need to focus on yourself through self-care. Taking care of yourself will help improve your overall mental and physical health and get rid of unhealthy habits. The first step toward self-care is making sure you are eating right, exercising enough, staying hydrated, and getting enough rest.

It can also present itself in the form of taking care of your physical appearance, such as getting your hair or nails done, taking a shower daily, taking care of your skin, meditation, relaxation, or hanging out with people you love. Self-care is about engaging in practices that help you feel rejuvenated. Make time for things that make you feel happy. Your quality of life may suffer if you are always putting other people's needs before your own. You have to find a balance between helping others and not sacrificing your well-being.

Try experimenting with different activities until you find those that make you happy and fulfilled.

Have a set routine to help you feel calmer if your mood is high or low and prepare you for a more stable mood

Routines provide structure and organization, which can significantly improve mental health. Therefore, it's important to create a routine that supports your general health and well-being. Routines can help reduce stress, which is a well-known trigger and aggravator of mood episodes. With a well-thought-out routine, you'll have peace of mind and more time to relax and do things you love, such as self-care. Think about creating a routine that incorporates things such as:

- Day-to-day activities (meal times and sleep times).
- Make time in your day for relaxation, mindfulness, hobbies, or social plans.
- If you are taking medication, take it at the same time every day to ensure consistency in the system.

Sleep schedules and good morning and night routines impact your alertness, motivation, energy levels, and emotional well-being. Create a consistent wake-up and sleeping routine so you can get better rest.

Having a consistent routine also helps build habits, and that can help you maintain good mental and physical health, excellent hygiene, as well as good relationships.

Engage in a purpose and create a sense of purpose. Evaluate your values and beliefs, review what is truly important to you, and set goals to match those ideals.

APPLICATION #4: SURROUND YOURSELF WITH POSITIVE INFLUENCE AND BUILD A SUPPORT NETWORK

When talking about a support network, think about:

- A family that has your back.
- Friends that you know will love and support you.
- Classmates who you never knew but have seen from afar.
- Mentors that you trust.
- Therapist, if you choose to see one.
- Finding those who can hold you accountable for your actions.

A bipolar disorder diagnosis can create a huge impact on family and other relationships because the diagnosis doesn't just affect the person, but everyone who loves and cares about them. Everyone around you will be strapped on this roller coaster for as long as the diagnosis lasts. But the good news is, the love and support of a family can help during difficult times when you are dealing with episodes. Families can also join in therapy sessions where they learn, heal, and support each other long-term. This way, together, you can find your way back to a loving, healthy, and fulfilling existence like it was before.

By surrounding yourself with people who love you, a supportive network, and positive influences, you can all get off that roller coaster caused by the intense mood swings, and back to a sense of stability. The hard thing about bipolar disorder is that there isn't a single mood for the people around you to adapt to. The extreme behaviors caused by the complex and opposite mood swings can be detrimental to relationships. For example, the impulsivity, arrogance associated with extreme self-confidence during manic episodes, irritability, and false feelings of indestructibility can be damaging to any form of relationship.

It could be impossible to get a word across edgewise, much less talk someone out of a dangerous idea while they are in a manic episode. You could turn on them pretty quickly when they don't agree with you.

Indeed, those are symptoms associated with manic episodes, but it can be frustrating nonetheless. In extreme cases, such situations can be outright danger- ous. The depressive end of the spectrum can also be just as dangerous and frustrating, such as when you are dealing with sleep and eating disorders, thoughts of self-harm, despair, emptiness, and hopelessness, or night-time insomnia and oversleeping during the day.

During a depressive state, you may have a hard time seeing outside yourself, and this can sometimes be seen as selfishness or narcissism. This can be upsetting for your family and support network. You may know that your obsession with sadness, guilt, and thoughts of self-harm hurts others, but in that state, you are less likely to understand the impact of your actions on others. You may be unable to do anything about your feelings except feel worse. This can be isolating, shutting out even those people who truly love and care about you. These extremes can lead to serious emotional strains, making it hard to create loving and supportive networks.

With that in mind, it's really important to be appreciative of family members who want to support you following a diagnosis. It's important to keep them close and be grateful for the support they offer. Positive influence and a strong support network can help with:

- Recognizing signs of a mood episode.
- Helping you look after yourself with routines and healthy diets.
- Listening/offering understanding or advice.
- Helping you process and reflect on what happened during manic episodes.
- Helping you plan for a crisis and when you are feeling unwell.

It is also important for your family to be involved in therapy, just like you are, particularly if you get feelings of "letting everyone down" during your manic/depressive episodes. You aren't letting anyone down. You need to know this and to see that you are surrounded by love and support. It's important to see that just like the symptoms of your disorder impact everyone around you, the therapy and treatment should also involve everyone.

APPLICATION #5: FACE YOUR FEARS AND STAND UP FOR YOURSELF

A little bit of fear is normal. In fact, fear is necessary and natural. Fear helps you protect yourself from risks instinctively. The natural flight or fight response enables you to recognize danger so you can make safer choices. But sometimes, especially when dealing with a mental health illness such as bipolar disorder, you may find yourself fearful of things that aren't life-threatening. Sometimes, when you are dealing with a mental health illness, you may have fears that the people around you may not understand. You may worry about not being yourself anymore or that if the issue is not well-managed, you may lose yourself completely.

Some people also get nervous about their diagnosis. They may wonder: *"What if something is very wrong? What will I do then?" "Could it be that I'm just going through a difficult time?" "Is all this necessary?"*

Fortunately, this doesn't have to happen. There are many helpful people and resources out there that can help you educate yourself about bipolar disorder, how to get the help you need, and what you can do to feel secure following a diagnosis. This isn't to imply that you will no longer have fears, but that you can and will have learned to manage them, and then, they'll be less impactful on your daily life. Try facing your fear and do something you may be scared to, such as:

- Volunteering in class.
- Speaking to a new classmate.
- Offering to hang out with friends.
- Eating out in public.
- Ordering food by yourself.
- Having a small conversation with your teacher.
- Sharing a highlight of your week with others.
- Joining building block groups that will help with relationship growth.
- Opening up to a family member or close friend about episodes (manic and depressive).
- Communicating various trigger warnings and early signs with people around you, as well as what will help you when you feel unwell.
- Feeling empowered and understanding that you are not powerless no matter how

down or out of control you or the situation
feels.

While avoiding your fears may be helpful in the
short term, complete avoidance can lead to anxiety.
When you avoid your fears, you train your brain to
think that you can't handle them. Learning to face
your fears, on the other hand, can help decrease
anxiety and train your brain that you are capable of
facing your fears.

The journal *Science* writes that our brains have to
experience frequent exposure to the very thing we are
scared of in order to overcome it. To experiment on
this, the experts used rodents. The rodents were
placed in tiny boxes and given mind shocks. Over
time, the same rodents were placed in the same little
boxes, but no shocks were administered. At first, the
rodents froze and were scared, just like the response
in the beginning. But after repeated exposure, they
got used to the box and learned to relax.[6]

Yes, research done on animals can't always be
applied to humans, but the concept behind facing your
fears aims to get the same outcome. You should face
your fears. You will not always conquer every fear
you have. But you have to think about the impact of
your fears on *your* life. Sit alone and think about your

fears. What are your fears stopping you from doing? Are these fears something you need to confront? Are they standing in your way of living a fulfilling life?

- Think about the advantages and disadvantages of not facing your fears. Write them down.
- Identify the advantages and disadvantages of facing your fears head-on.
- Write down the positive things that may happen and what you may achieve when you finally overcome those fears.
- Go over your list again and think about what you want to do next.

If you've been diagnosed with bipolar disorder, know that you are not alone, and your case isn't unique. Millions of teens all over the world are dealing with bipolar disorder and other complex mental health illnesses. Remember that you don't have to go through it alone. Your family is right there with you, your friends love you, and healthcare providers with lots of experience in the field are more than happy to help whenever you need them to. There are many resources, online and offline, that you can take advantage of to understand what bipolar disorder is. Always remember to reach out to loved ones and professionals whenever you need support, or you don't understand something.

Together, we can create a more understanding, less judgmental, and empathetic society that empowers teens like you with bipolar disorder. Mental health or any diagnosis isn't something to be ashamed of. It is okay to talk about it and seek support from others openly when you are struggling. After all, you aren't alone in this. Everyone is here, open and willing to experience the journey with you.

CHAPTER 8
LIVING LIFE TO THE FULLEST

No one wants to be told that they have a mental health disorder. Tell someone they have diabetes, mobility issues, heart disease, or other "normal" illnesses, and nine times out of ten, they'll handle the news better than hearing that they may have a mental health illness. Moreover, people like to think that when someone is living with a mental health disorder, they must be or should always be miserable. They should stay home, hidden away from others. This stigma surrounding mental health needs to stop.

First, mental illness, in whichever form it comes in, is never linear. Your feelings can change from one moment to the next, day to day, week to week, and so on. When it comes to bipolar disorder, for example, you may find yourself struggling on certain days and being happy on other days. There are days you may not want to get out of bed or even take a shower, but there are days you'll wake up and go out with friends and family despite how you feel. You will have great days when you want to go out, socialize, dance, and laugh with your friends. Sadly, the stigma surrounding mental illnesses that those with mental disorders encounter, can stop them from living those moments to the fullest.

Many people living with mental illnesses admit that they've often worried that people will think they are faking it if they see them happy or smiling. When they take breaks from school or work because of their mental health, they worry about someone seeing them doing something "fun" and will not understand that they might be having a good day. People will see those days. But they'll not see the bad days when you are stuck in bed, hearing voices, and having thoughts of self-harm.

But you have to understand that you deserve to be happy. You shouldn't feel bad for times of happiness and relief. If anything, you should try to pursue happiness, live life to the fullest, and enjoy the great moments when you can. Yes, you can live life to the fullest, even though you are living with bipolar disorder. This chapter will offer various ways to live life to the fullest. This definition can be applied differently to each person, but the overall concept will be presented here.

A lot of teens will keep to themselves about struggling with bipolar disorder until someone else brings it up. This disorder should not be something you have to find ways around, but instead, it should be something you deal with and break out of. You can have peace and solace in knowing that you are not the only one dealing with this, and there have been many others who were in the same steps as you, but are now free and healed of this disorder.

IT IS OKAY TO EMBRACE DISCOMFORT AND BREAK THIS CYCLE OF BIPOLAR DISORDER

People tend to avoid discomfort because they love to feel comfortable. This is a natural part of being human, and that's how the human brain works. We love to stay away from things that we perceive as uncomfortable. But every meaningful thing in life that helps you grow to become a better person, has a certain degree of discomfort. For example, if you want to be better at public speaking, you'll have to do the uncomfortable thing such as speaking to an audience. You may experience performance anxiety in the process, but the experience—will ultimately make you better at public speaking.

But the more you avoid discomfort, the less likely you are to grow and change. When dealing with bipolar disorder, discomfort may arise when you:

- Are in an unknown situation.
- Avoid things that are anxiety-inducing (and stress-inducing).
- Avoid any associated feelings that arise due to manic or depressive episodes.
- Learn to set schedules/routines and stick with them.
- Learn to surround yourself with positive influence and a strong support system.
- Continue to face your fears and stand up for yourself.

Still, you have to embrace the discomfort to grow. When you are dealing with something uncomfortable and you find ways to overcome it, you will be in a position to handle similar uncomfortable situations in the future. This will build your confidence over time. The more confident you are in your ability to over-come challenges that bring discomfort, the more open you'll be to taking risks. So, how can you do this?

Pursue discomfort, little by little

Start small. Expose yourself to discomfort voluntarily. You can try:

- Waking up at least 10 minutes earlier.
- Taking a cold shower.
- Eating food you'd never try.
- Hanging out in a place you'd never go to.

Be willing to be uncomfortable

Be open to embracing discomfort instead of avoiding it. This doesn't mean you are now comfortable with the experience or that you love it. It simply means that you are willing to tolerate it.

- Breathe in and out. Breathe into that uncomfortable feeling.
- Normalize the discomfort. It's okay to experience discomfort when taking risks.
- Name the feeling. For example, *"This is discomfort. I am feeling uncomfortable."*

Allow the feeling to present itself. Allow and embrace the discomfort when it manifests itself.

Work on a mindset shift

Your mindset is your perception of the things happening around you and in your life. If you view discomfort as a negative thing, you'll most likely try to avoid it. If you view discomfort as something you need to grow in, you'll be more willing to tolerate and embrace it. How can you achieve a mindset shift? Try:

- To set goals based on your values.
- Learn to take perspective.
- Meditate.
- Journal.
- Get curious.

Therapy

You can also get help from a professional. A therapist can help you learn a new habit or skill. Through therapy, you can explore your relationship with discomfort and learn to embrace it. Talking to a therapist is a great way to learn what you are uncomfortable with and why and how you can embrace discomfort. Once you've learned to embrace discomfort and tolerate it, you are well on your way to living your life to the fullest.

HOW TO LIVE YOUR LIFE TO THE FULLEST

Find ways to be happy

Each person is entitled to happiness and deserves to experience that in their own life. This happiness will come from the way you view and react to situations. You have to care for yourself, as you will never be able to change the way others act or think around you. You deserve to live a normal life and not be deprived of experiences or happiness due to a disorder that feels unbearable. There are so many things you can do to be happy. Try doing the following:

- Find and partake in an activity that brings you joy, e.g., music, exercise, or watching movies.
- Spend time with friends (venture out and make new ones).
- Spend time with family (create some new memories together).

- Get a pet that you can care for, sign up to care for one, or volunteer at your local animal shelter.
- Read a good book, support new authors, or volunteer at the local library.
- Listen to music or attend a concert.
- Travel somewhere (domestic or international), find someone to go with you, or go solo.
- Volunteer at your city outreach programs (homeless shelters, food kitchens, children's homes, etc.).
- Literally anything that keeps you occupied and that you enjoy doing.

Attitude is everything

A positive attitude is good for your physical and mental health. Your attitude toward your diagnosis, healthcare providers, medication, the family and friends supporting you, therapy, and this illness in general will either make or break you. Thinking positive and happy thoughts will play a big role in living your life to the fullest.

Change your mindset about bipolar disorder

I believe the first step toward living your life to the fullest is changing your mindset about bipolar disorder and other mental illnesses in general. Most often, people with mental illnesses struggle with low self-esteem. Some even hate their lives and the fact that they are ill. This is a destructive outlook, and changing it is the real battle. If you learn to think of this disorder differently, you'll feel differently, too.

For example, stop saying, "*My illness,*" "*MY,*" "*My depression!*" It's enough that others label people with mental illnesses. You don't need to do that to yourself as well. In doing this, you lose every semblance of who you are in the labels. You are more than your diagnosis. Think about who you used to be before the bipolar disorder diagnosis. Were you good at art? Sports? Public speaking? Music? Remember the things you loved doing and gravitate more toward them, along with the things that made you happy.

With the right attitude, this illness will be nothing more than a bump in the road. It won't be something that defines you for the rest of your life. It won't be an illness you have to deal with for the rest of your life. It is not a death sentence.

Reframe your thoughts

We touched a little bit on how and why you should reframe your thoughts in chapter 7, but this process also has a big part in how you can start to live your days to the fullest. Think of something else other than bipolar disorder. You had dreams before this, right? What goals did you have? What kind of things did you want to achieve? Or do? Just because you have bipolar disorder doesn't mean you have no future. Your future is still as bright as it used to be before this diagnosis.

But first, you must have a healthy attitude toward your diagnosis—the treatment, medication, and your support system. You have to eat right, go to sleep on time, and think healthy thoughts. Think of ways you can be of service to others. Get your mind off yourself, and you'll be surprised by how much better you think and feel.

If you force yourself to think happy thoughts from the moment you wake up, everything in your day changes. For example, before you get out of bed, sit upright and tell yourself out loud, *"Today is going to be an amazing day. No matter what happens, good or bad, I'll not let anything ruin my day. I am a happy, healthy person. I can handle everything that comes my way today."* Don't give up! Don't give in! You are stronger, much stronger than you think.

Live for the good days

We all have good and bad days, but when you are living with bipolar disorder, the good days may seem fleeting. When you have that sense of stability, no matter how short it is, appreciate it. That social event that you were invited to months ago that you were thinking of turning down, try it. That dinner date you wrote in your calendar, don't think twice about going now.

Going out and socializing is a great way to maintain a healthy mind and spirit. When you are in the middle of a bad episode, you can look back at the great days and know that they always come back. You will see that it's just a matter of time before you feel better again, and this will give you hope.

Write down the good things you did during your great days and put them somewhere safe, like in a jar. When you aren't feeling good, grab a few slips from your jar and read them out loud. Reading about the things you did when times were good will give you great comfort. This may also remind you of what you are capable of, so you can look forward to the good days once again.

Understand your limits

A significant part of managing your mental illness is understanding your limits. For example, if you know coffee increases your anxiety or interferes with your medication, stick with something that works for you. A soft drink would be a great alternative in such a case. True, you are working towards living your best life, but you shouldn't overestimate how much you are capable of handling. This could cause problems later.

Trying to fit everything in or please everyone may drain you. If you don't feel like going out, don't do it. Instead, try to rest. Plus, having fun and living your life to the fullest doesn't always mean going out. It could be as simple as watching your favorite movie on your sofa, in the comfort of your own home. Ultimately, this is about knowing when you've had enough. Your health should always come first because that's more important than doing too much or impressing others.

Don't hold on to the guilt

Mental illness carries a lot of guilt and stigma. You may struggle to break a habit because it's closely intertwined with your illness. Still, you have to permit yourself to live your life to the fullest. Just because you have bipolar disorder doesn't mean you have to be or act like you are miserable every day. Your life isn't just limited to bipolar disorder. Give yourself a break sometimes and enjoy your life.

You can talk about your feelings of guilt with a therapist, family, or close friends. They can help you understand and process those negative thought patterns. If you are still struggling to do this, try Dialectical Behavior Therapy (DBT), or Cognitive Behavioral Therapy (CBT), already mentioned in chapter 7. These therapies are good at challenging and changing negative thought patterns.

Lean on friends and family

Find your support system and lean on them. This should be a small group of dependable people that you can always talk to. These people know you well. They know that you are okay on certain days and struggle with others, and they understand you. Because they care about your well-being, they will love and support you during the good and bad days just as much.

This list is by no means endless or exhaustive. You know yourself best, and you know the things that make you happy. Go out in pursuit of those things, and don't stop at anything until you find them. You only have one life to live, so make the most of it. Tomorrow is never promised; therefore, do what you can today. Bipolar disorder causes teens to have, accept, and live with feelings of isolation, being alone, and living in pain. This shouldn't be the case. Find your tribe and people who love you, and have fun with them. You can do it.

CONCLUSION

Bipolar disorder is a unique and complex mood disorder that can lead to intense emotional changes. Chapters 1 and 2 highlight the different moods, symptoms, and challenges that you may struggle with as a teen living with bipolar disorder. Although bipolar disorder can be challenging to live with, it's possible to live a more balanced and happy life when you make the right lifestyle adjustments.

Getting the right and early diagnosis is the first step towards overcoming bipolar disorder and living a happy life. What's more, you have to accept that there is life after the diagnosis and start treatment and therapy sooner. By doing this, you'll be able to cope with the treatment better. Once you start treatment and perhaps even therapy, you'll realize that your symptoms are easier to manage. The Depression and

Bipolar Support Alliance (DBSA), reports that people living with bipolar disorder can live happy, normal lives, just like everyone else.[1]

Still, there is a reason why this question is asked, and the answer can sometimes be complicated. Sometimes, if you've experienced a manic episode in the past, you may be concerned when you feel happy, thinking that it could be the start of another manic episode. For this reason, you may feel stuck, unable to let yourself be genuinely happy. But instead of looking at any sign of happiness as a warning, the DBSA suggests that you learn about your triggers and the warning signs of an imminent episode.[1]

You can go back to chapter 2 and refresh your memory on symptoms, warning signs, and root causes of bipolar disorder so that you have better insight. With that, you can feel safer and at ease when you feel happy or sad, in a "normal sense," and watch out for other complex and specific signs such as irritability, withdrawal, or anxiety, which may either indicate mania or depressive episodes.

Chapter 7 highlights the importance of applying the tips presented to your current situation in your daily life, and how you can find ways to identify your triggers and early warning signs. When you understand your triggers and early warning signs, you'll know when you are simply happy or sad, or when you are dealing with an episode. Knowledge is literally power in this sense. You must be informed and arm yourself with the right knowledge to overcome this complex disorder.

More importantly, it is worth noting that if you have been prescribed bipolar disorder medication, it may make you feel dull or flat.[2] The whole idea behind treatment is not to make you feel emotionless. If this happens, make sure to let your healthcare provider know. Also, you have to understand that the lifestyle changes suggested in chapters 5, 7, and 8 will affect different people in different ways. You may respond to these changes differently because what works for someone else may not always work for you and vice versa.

It's best to find and stick with what works for you. It's also important to take medication exactly as prescribed, no ifs, no buts. You shouldn't stop taking your medication, even when you feel better. This is just a sign that you are on the right path and the treatment is working as it should. Above all, continue taking advantage of the resources around you to learn more about bipolar disorder and hold your support system as close as possible. By doing this, you will set yourself up for success, which in return, will lead to a healthier, happier life.

Thank you so much for reading this book. If you found any of the things discussed here helpful, please leave a positive review on the platform from which you obtained this copy. That way, other teens with bipolar disorder will get to read this book and benefit from its teachings and findings too.

Thank you.

Your friend,

Natasha Rae Simmons

REFERENCES

References

Introduction:

1. American Psychiatric Association. (n.d.). *What are bipolar disorders?* https://www.psychiatry.org/patients-families/bipolar-disorders/what-are-bipolar-disorders

2. Robinson, L., Segal, J., & Smith, M. (n.d.). *Helping someone with bipolar disorder.* HelpGuide.org. https://www.helpguide.org/articles/bipolar-disorder/helping-someone-with-bipolar-disorder.htm

Chapter 1:

1. *Bipolar disorder.* (2017). National Alliance On Mental Illness. https://www.nami.org/about-mental-illness/mental-health-conditions/bipolar-disorder

2. Purse, M. (2022). *Why did manic depression become bipolar disorder?* Verywell Mind. https://www.verywellmind.com/why-did-manic-depression-become-bipolar-disorder-379822

3. Mayo Clinic Staff. (2022). *Bipolar disorder.* Mayo Clinic. https://www.mayoclinic.org/diseases-conditions/bipolar-disorder/symptoms-causes/syc-20355955

4. Cambridge Dictionary. (n.d.). *Mood.* In *Cambridge Dictionary.* https://dictionary.cambridge.org/dictionary/english/mood

5. Ahmad, S. (n.d.). *Bipolar disorder: A diagnostic chameleon.* Samoon Ahmad, MD. https://samoonmd.com/bipolar-disorder-a-diagnostic-chameleon

6. Arnold, L. M. (2003). *Gender differences in bipolar disorder.* National Library of Medicine. https://pubmed.ncbi.nlm.nih.gov/14563100

7. Robinson, L., Segal, J., & Smith, M. (2024). *Helping someone*

with bipolar disorder. HelpGuide.org.
https://www.helpguide.org/articles/bipolar-disorder/helping-someone-with-bipolar-disorder.htm

8. *Hypomania: What is it, comparison vs mania, symptoms & treatment.* (2021). Cleveland Clinic. https://my.clevelandclinic.org/health/diseases/21774-hypomania

9. Dailey, M., & Saadabadi, A. (2023). *Mania.* National Library of Medicine. https://pubmed.ncbi.nlm.nih.gov/29630220

10. Roland, J. (2022). *What's the difference between cyclothymia and bipolar disorder?* Healthline. https://www.healthline.com/health/bipolar/cyclothymia-vs-bipolar

11. Mayo Clinic Staff. (2022). *Cyclothymia (cyclothymic disorder).* Mayo Clinic. https://www.mayoclinic.org/diseases-conditions/cyclothymia/symptoms-causes/syc-20371275

Chapter 2:

1. Farnsworth, C. (2023). *4 common bipolar disorder misdiagnoses.* MedicalNewsToday. https://www.medicalnewstoday.com/articles/common-bipolar-disorder-misdiagnoses

2. University of Missouri-Columbia. (2009). *Young adults may outgrow bipolar disorder.* www.sciencedaily.com/releases/2009/09/090929141530.htm

3. *Bipolar disorder causes.* (n.d.). Black Dog Institute. https://www.blackdoginstitute.org.au/resources-support/bipolar-disorder/causes

4. Purse, M. (2021). *Understanding the causes of bipolar disorder.* Verywell Mind. https://www.verywellmind.com/what-causes-bipolar-disorder-378711

5. Scott, J. A. (2023). *Why bipolar disorder is often wrongly diagnosed.* Everyday Health. https://www.everydayhealth.com/news/why-bipolar-disorder-is-often-misdiagnosed

6. *Which neurotransmitter plays a role in bipolar disorder?* (n.d). Vinmec International Hospital. https://www.vinmec.-

com/en/news/health-news/general-health-check/which-neuro-transmitter-plays-a-role-in-bipolar-disorder

Chapter 3:

1. Axelson, D., Birmaher, B., Douaihy, A., Garcia, M., Goldstein, T. R., Krantz, M., Merranko, J., Rodriguez, C., & Sobel, L. (2016). Medication adherence among adolescents with bipolar disorder. *Journal of Child and Adolescent Psychopharmacology, 26(10), 864–872.* https://doi.org/10.1089/cap.2016.0030

2. Gold, A., & Sylvia, L. (2016). The role of sleep in bipolar disorder. *Nature and Science of Sleep, 8, 207-214.* https://doi.org/10.2147/NSS.S85754

3. Kemp, D. E. (2014). Managing the side effects associated with commonly used treatments for bipolar depression. *Journal of Affective Disorders, 169, S34–S44.* https://doi.org/10.1016/S0165-0327(14)70007-2

4. Scaccia, A. (2019). *How to recognize and treat bipolar disorder in teens.* Healthline. https://www.healthline.com/health/bipolar-disorder/bipolar-disorder-in-teens

5. Cherney, K. (2018). *Psychomotor retardation (impairment).* Healthline. https://www.healthline.com/health/psychomotor-retardation

6. Almeida, J. R., Clark, L., Hassel, S., Klein, C., LaBarbara, E. J., Maalouf, F. T., Phillips, M. L., Sahakian, B. J., & Versace, A. (2010). Impaired sustained attention and executive dysfunction: Bipolar disorder versus depression-specific markers of affective disorders. *Neuropsychologia, 48(6), 1862–1868.* https://doi.org/10.1016/j.neuropsychologia.2010.02.015

Chapter 4:

1. Morin, A. (2024). *Therapy for teens: Types, uses, benefits, and what to expect.* Verywell Mind. https://www.verywellmind.com/therapy-for-teens-2610410

2. *Bipolar disorder.* (2022). Mind. https://www.mind.org.uk/infor-

mation-support/types-of-mental-health-problems/bipolar-disor-der/causes-of-bipolar

3. *Sleep problems in teens.* (n.d.). UCLA Health. https://www.ucla-health.org/medical-services/sleep-disorders/patient-resources/patient-education/sleep-and-teens

4. Pugle, M. (2022). *Bipolar disorder raises your risk for these 4 mental health conditions, too.* EverydayHealth. https://www.everydayhealth.com/bipolar-disorder/bipolar-disor-der-raises-your-risk-for-these-mental-health-conditions-too

5. *Which neurotransmitter plays a role in bipolar disorder?* (n.d.). Vinmec International Hospital. https://www.vinmec.-com/en/news/health-news/general-health-check/which-neuro-transmitter-plays-a-role-in-bipolar-disorder

6. Familydoctor.org Editorial Staff. (2023). *Talking to your doctor about your mental health.* Familydoctor.org. https://familydoc-tor.org/talking-to-your-doctor-about-your-mental-health

7. Mayo Clinic Staff. (2022). *Bipolar disorder*. Mayo Clinic. https://www.mayoclinic.org/diseases-conditions/bipolar-disor-der/symptoms-causes/syc-20355955

8. WebMD. (n.d.). *Lifestyle changes to help bipolar depression.* https://www.webmd.com/bipolar-disorder/ss/slideshow-bipolar-depression-lifestyle-changes

Chapter 6:

1. Mayo Clinic Staff. (2023). *Chronic stress puts your health at risk*. Mayo Clinic. https://www.mayoclinic.org/healthy-life-style/stress-management/in-depth/stress/art-20046037

2. *Mood and sleep.* (2022). Better Health Channel. https://www.bet-terhealth.vic.gov.au/health/healthyliving/Mood-and-sleep

3. Mayo Clinic Staff. (2022). *Exercise and stress: Get moving to manage stress*. Mayo Clinic. https://www.mayoclin-ic.org/healthy-lifestyle/stress-management/in-depth/exercise-and-stress/art-20044469

4. *Dialectical behaviour therapy (DBT).* (2024). Mind. https://www.mind.org.uk/information-support/drugs-and-treatments/talking-therapy-and-counselling/dialectical-behaviour-therapy-dbt

Chapter 7:

1. *Nutrition and healthy eating.* (n.d.). Healthy People 2030. https://health.gov/healthypeople/objectives-and-data/browse-objectives/nutrition-and-healthy-eating

2. Rothstein, L., & Stromme, D. (n.d.). *Celebrate the small stuff.* University of Minnesota Extension. https://extension.umn.edu/two-you-video-series/celebrate-small-stuff

3. *Dialectical behaviour therapy (DBT). (2024).* Mind. https://www.mind.org.uk/information-support/drugs-and-treatments/talking-therapy-and-counselling/dialectical-behaviour-therapy-dbt

4. Mayo Clinic Staff. (2023). Exercise: *7 benefits of regular physical activity.* Mayo Clinic. https://www.mayoclinic.org/healthy-lifestyle/fitness/in-depth/exercise/art-20048389

5. Damiano, S. R., & Paxton, S. J. (2017). Chapter Eight - The Development of Body Image and Weight Bias in Childhood. *Advances in Child Development and Behavior, JAI, Volume 52, Pages 269-298.* https://doi.org/10.1016/bs.acdb.2016.10.006

6. Morin, A. (2023). *How to face your fears when you want to tackle them head-on.* Verywell Mind. https://www.verywell-mind.com/healthy-ways-to-face-your-fears-4165487

Conclusion:

1. Simon, G. (n.d.). *Can a person with bipolar disorder ever be truly happy? Are my periods of happiness just mania?* Depression and Bipolar Support Alliance. https://www.dbsalliance.org/education/ask-the-doc/can-a-person-with-bipolar-disorder-ever-be-truly-happy

2. Robinson, L., Segal, J., & Smith, M. (2024). *Bipolar disorder*

REFERENCES

medication guide. HelpGuide.org.
https://www.helpguide.org/articles/bipolar-disorder/bipolar-medication-guide.htm